THE VIOLENCE
OF LITERACY

THE VIOLENCE
OF LITERACY

◆

J. ELSPETH STUCKEY

BOYNTON/COOK PUBLISHERS
HEINEMANN
PORTSMOUTH, NEW HAMPSHIRE

Boynton/Cook Publishers, Inc.
A Subsidiary of
Heinemann Educational Books, Inc.
361 Hanover Street   Portsmouth, NH 03801-3959
Offices and agents throughout the world

Library of Congress Cataloging-in-Publication Data

Stuckey, J. Elspeth.
  The violence of literacy / J. Elspeth Stuckey.
    p.   cm.
  Includes bibliographical references.
  ISBN 0-86709-270-X
    1. Literacy—United States. 2. Education—Social aspects—United
  States. 3. United States–Social conditions. I. Title.
  LC151.S78   1991
    302.2′244–dc20   90-41385
                                                               CIP

Designed by Jenny Greenleaf.
Printed in the United States of America.
91 92 93 94 95 9 8 7 6 5 4 3 2 1

CONTENTS

INTRODUCTION

In the United States we live the mythology of a classless society. We believe our society provides equal opportunities for all and promises success to those who work hard to achieve it. We believe the key to achievement is education, and we believe the heart of education is literacy. In a society bound by such a mythology, our views about literacy are our views about political economy and social opportunity.

This study does not agree with our beliefs. It surveys the ideology, theory, and practice of literacy in an attempt to explode the mythology and question its foundations. It argues that usual speculations about the nature and need for literacy are misguided. These speculations are wrong because the assumptions about economic and social forces on which they are based are faulty. Literacy itself can be understood only in its social and political context, and that context, once the mythology has been stripped away, can be seen as one of entrenched class structure in which those who have power have a vested interest in keeping it.

This study also finds that many current practices in research, theory making, and teaching are not just misguided but are destructive as well. Far from engineering freedom, our current approaches to literacy corroborate other social practices that prevent freedom and limit opportunity. In a self-serving society such as ours, our efforts in education too often only reinforce the strategies of self-service.

The current high profile of literacy is symptomatic of a speedy, ruthless transition from an industrial to an information-based economy. This economic shift accentuates literacy's role in economic growth, class structure, and social estrangement. Literacy, to be sure, is a powerful, unique technology. Yet literacy remains a human invention contained by social contract, and the maintenance of that contract in education betrays our ideas of humanity as surely as our use of literacy enforces them. Are we helping those in need of economic and social opportunity, or those (including ourselves) who wish to maintain their own economic and social advantage?

These are the issues and questions that inform the analysis that follows. These are the questions that enlarge the topic of literacy beyond the narrow scope of teaching techniques and national cries of alarm over the high rates of illiteracy in the United States. The issues surrounding literacy are complex, but they are not mysterious. This study seeks to clarify them.

CHAPTER ONE

LITERACY AND SOCIAL CLASS

◆

The idea of a class structure is uncomfortable for many Americans. It is anathema to American educators. Mortimer Adler, author of *The Paideia Proposal: An Educational Manifesto*, demonstrates this discomfort when he says of the United States, "We are politically a classless society. Our citizenry as a whole is our ruling class. We should, therefore, be an educationally classless society" (5). Adler is classically American in his optimism.

What we must understand is our educational investment in egalitarianism. The investment is the best and the worst indicator of what education does in America. It depends on an idea of class that claims to be either inoperative or easily dismantled. Perhaps American sociology provides our best vehicle for understanding and scrutinizing the sympatico distaste for class among American educators and American citizenry.

In some of the early sociological research conducted in the United States, Robert and Helen Merrell Lynd found it unnecessary to classify more than two groups in the population of a town they called Middletown, USA, in 1924 (*Middletown* 22–23). These were the Business class and the Working class. By 1935, however, a follow-up study produced six classes (six becomes the number of classes subject to wide standardization in subsequent sociological, federal, and educational research). Yet the Lynds reported that class structure remained an unpopular idea. They said of Middletown:

> It is more congenial to the mood of the city, proud of its traditions of democratic equality, to think of the lines of cleavage within its social systems as based not upon class differences but rather upon the entirely spontaneous and completely individual and personal predilections of the 12,500 families who compose its population. (*Middletown in Transition* 60)

The Lynds sought in Middletown to discover the peculiarities of American class; they experienced partial success by locating it in a denial of class distinctions.

The American propensity to deny class is recognized by non-Americans, too. In 1944, Gunnar Myrdal described the prototypical American as one who "investigates his own faults, puts them on record, and shouts them from the housetops, adding the most severe recriminations against himself, including the accusation of hypocrisy" (21). Myrdal was specifically concerned with how Americans deal with the problems of racism, problems that others subsume under the construct of class (Lewontin, et al. 26, 119–129; Wilkins 437). Smiling optimism, which Myrdal calls "bright fatalism . . . unmatched in the rest of the Western World," somehow both captivates and confuses the American soul (xix). Even staunch empirical sociologists are forced to admit that "although systematic evidence is lacking," Americans "are less class-conscious than Europeans" (Kahl 174).

There is another side to this peculiar notion, however, and that is how such optimism persists in the face of contradiction. Sociology textbooks are compelled to embrace this American idea of classlessness while painting an opposite picture. Some groups, for example, do seem to constitute a "ragged bottom margin" in which poor whites and blacks fit most frequently (Kahl 60). W. Lloyd Warner, in an early-1940s study of a town he named Yankeeville, identified a lowest of the low classes, which he called "the 'lulus' or disrespectable and often slovenly people . . . who waited for public relief." These groups were composed of the unskilled and uneducated.

How could the failure to benefit from an optimistic system, one that denied the possibility of "class" failure, be explained? The answer sociologists often give belies the difficulty of the situation and capitalizes on it. This answer claims that the belief in classlessness is rooted in the dominant attitude of well-being and usually rests on the American faith in individual strength and willpower; citizens get what they achieve. There is, for example, the myth of the loner, the American individualist who stakes out his territory and defines his own worth. Richard Sennett in *The Hidden Injuries of Class* backhands the notion this way: "If you don't belong to the society, society can't hurt you" (55). Sennett's knowledge, of course, is to the contrary. Nevertheless, confidence in the "life, liberty, and pursuit of happiness" mentality is pervasive. It explains what is perhaps most insidious and distressing about the American system of class—the willingness, if not the felt need, of disfranchised citizens to rationalize their inequality. Michael Harrington in *The New American Poverty* writes:

> If you ask the unemployed steelworkers in the Mon [Monongahela] Valley about their social class, they do not have a moment's hesitation. "We pay the taxes and take care of the kids and go out for beer and pizza," a steelworker's wife—an activist in her own right—insisted. "We're middle class." Or, as Douglas Fraser, the former president of the auto worker's union, put it, these are "working people of the middle class." (40)

Harrington calls this description a "sociological contradiction and a psychological fact in a country where the working class exists but cannot say its own name" (40). The issue is not distaste for class but how distaste obscures class.

It is axiomatic to say that occupation is the salient marker of class. Yet, in American sociology, occupation has been virtually explained away. Although historical class definitions have placed occupation at the center of class lives, American sociologists have treated occupation as only one variable of class. Occupation is a sort of leading indicator. Kahl calls occupation a "convenient" variable. Its convenience lies in its predictive powers of other, presumably more accurate, variables. Among other things, Kahl says that occupation predicts a man's education; it suggests the type of associates he comes in contact with; it tells something of the contribution he makes to the community welfare; it hints at the degree of his authority over other people (53).

These other features are understood to occupy positions of parity with work (and utterly ignore issues of gender and race). Six of these features emerge to pattern the fabric of daily life; it is important to summarize them not simply because they yield familiar descriptions of class and human hierarchy in America, but also because the familiarity is embedded in the system of American education.

These six standardized indicators or variables of class are (a) personal prestige, (b) occupation, (c) possessions, (d) interaction, (e) class consciousness, and (f) value orientation. The most "conspicuous" manifestation of class behavior, however, is difficult to pin to any one variable. That behavior is "consumption"—how people spend their money. Gerard Lenski asserts that the most important question in class research is "who gets what and why" (3); the "what," of course, is the consumed—possessions, values, and educational rites among them.

These variables constitute only baselines, however. They are augmented with the quantification of qualities—such as prestige—and the assimilation of these quantifications into longstanding measures such as census categories. Thus, Warner in the Yankeeville study grew to distrust his original benchmark of economic status as the determinant of class position and expanded the study to include "a vast collection of data"; Warner concluded that the classes of Yankeeville were rarely confused given information about "education, occupation, wealth, income, family, intimate friends, clubs and fraternities, as well as . . . manners, speech, and general outward behavior." In a crunch, he decided, "repeated home invitation[s] to dinner" identified class equality between persons.

The value to sociologists of these procedures (whose questionableness is debated long and often but whose familiarity cannot be disputed) is summary. On the basis of numerous studies such as those of the Lynds and Warner, analysts presume to draw a six-tiered strata of American society, the "ideal" rather than actual types that result from meticulous addition, averaging, and, obviously, bias. Thus, Kahl, for example, identifies top halves and bottom halves of society. In the top half are the "graceful livers" and the "career-inspired"; in the bottom are the "apathetic." The "graceful livers" exhibit more than anything else an "attitude" toward life that places them above the rest. They are capable of companionship, are versatile in hobbies, can "talk of music or politics or business." In the next notch down, the "career-inspired" citizens expend a good bit of their time at work, albeit successfully: "Their whole way of life—their consumption behavior, their sense of accomplishment and respectability, the source of much of their prestige with others—depends upon success in a career. The husband's career becomes the central social fact for the family." This class is also convinced that its success has grown out of "greater talent and greater devotion to jobs" than class members of other ilk. The "apathetic," on the other hand, unlike the "respectable" middle classes, suffer from fatalism. Entire families live in one room. The "apathetic" drift from job to job and have few skills. Unfortunately for them, they also suffer from "inferior biological stock ... an inescapable handicap." Kahl concludes this taxonomy by admitting that there is variation from state to state in the union and "a great deal of controversy over detail," yet he believes that class in America can be pretty well delineated and understood within these terms (184–217).

In a country whose most recent preoccupation with the yuppie—not to mention the sociobiologist—tends to confirm rather than contradict the penchant to both create and valorize relationships between conversational prowess and genes, Kahl's description is hardly surprising. One obvious problem with descriptions such as Kahl's, grievous in its clarity, however, is that they overstate their own warrants. The second problem, of course, is that the warrants are wrong. There is the dilemma, for example, of what sociologist Gerard Lenski calls "status inconsistency" within the hierarchy (87). A black doctor, for example, is not highly esteemed by mill workers or visited by upper class whites. A pipefitter who lives next door to a schoolteacher rates twice the pay and half the social esteem (Sennett 35; Heath, *Ways* 34). This sort of disparity threatens the integrity of sociological design. So, something must be done.

A palliative to these lapses comes in the form of social ethnography, an alternative research procedure that has grown in esteem in the last decade. Ethnography has always accompanied empirical research, but its nature, until recently, has been more openly ulterior and its use sporadic. Unfortunately, its results reinforce rather than question usual sociological assumptions. To do typical ethnography, for example, a researcher identifies a type of class member, then seeks out representatives whom the researcher can address questions to, spend time with, and observe.

In the late 1950s and mid-1960s, several well-known studies of Southern social classes employed ethnographic methods.

The Millways of Kent provides a useful example. In it, the ethnographer requests from informants descriptions of members of the community. A town informant supplies a description of the males who work in the mill, men who

> do so many hours of work in the mill, walk down to their favorite hangout spots to sit around and talk, get "high" on weekends, and then go home to beat their wives or do whatever they are accustomed to doing. (Morland 176)

A town doctor corroborates the idea that mill folks are the "dirtiest, nastiest people in the world" (Morland 176). This testimony was useful as it often explained away statistical deviations within class hierarchies. The upshot is that the method determines not merely what dominant people look at and see but also what they do not see.

A more recent example of this, a groundbreaking linguistic ethnography by Shirley Brice Heath, simply has to rise above its tacit assumptions about class. In the study of three linguistic groups, class consists of an inundation of peremptory features, features that are ingrained in class-unconscious Americans. Thus, class is located in descriptions of clothes, home decor, grass in yards, club membership, and so on. Women from the mill village wear polyester pants suits with unpressed seams; town women buy their polyester garments with more finished detail. Within homes, plastic flowers, linear furniture arrangements, and "double portraits of Coretta and Martin Luther King often with small school photos of the household's children stuck in the bottom of the same frame" differentiate class from class (*Ways* 30–39, 55).

The startling analysis of the study suggests the correlations of such minutiae with the linguistic success—or lack of it—in schools of children from each linguistic group. The limitation of the undertaking is that it is hampered by a traditional notion of class. As a result, the solution to linguistic inequality would appear to be to adopt middle class style, since middle class style is the arbiter of equal opportunity.

Nothing could be farther from the truth—especially linguistically—yet we are left with few alternatives in the current situation. That is why it is necessary to understand how traditional notions of class have come to inform so much of our work. Indeed, it is necessary in this case to understand how early disciplinary efforts lost an initiative that, if retained, may well have helped rather than hindered the English approach to literacy.

In early sociological work, such as that of the Lynds, the discovery that peculiar habits and situations cleaved to the self-sufficient, the working, and the entrepreneurial members of a small town had its value. The machine, as the Lynds observed, made a tremendous impact in the years from 1890 to 1910, and it was that impact they sought to understand (*Middletown* 5). The two distinct classes revealed in the Lynds' early study at the turn of the century were based on the work that the people did and the relationships between those types of work within the town. The Lynds were unequivocal:

> While an effort will be made to make clear at certain points variant behavior within these two groups, it is after all this division into working class and business class that constitutes the outstanding cleavage in Middletown. (*Middletown* 23)

They made a fundamentally important statement to the effect that "the mere fact of being born upon one or the other side of the watershed" most significantly determined a person's activity "all day long through one's life." Working-class people, the Lynds described, "get their living primarily by addressing things." They work on or beside machines. Members of the business class, on the other hand, dwell with others of their kind, addressing "their activities predominantly to people in the selling or promotion of things, services, or ideas." Also, the members of this class are the owners or writers of contracts, credit, education, "nonmaterial" things, and they control the negotiations among all townspeople; they control the institutions of negotiation (*Middletown* 31).

For a seminal understanding of the importance and nature of literacy to class structure, the Lynds could hardly have drawn a clearer picture.

Yet, despite this realization of the basis for class differences, by 1935 the Lynds trade two classes for the standard six, and the identification of these classes loses its affinity with work. Rather than a relationship to and from machines and human negotiation, these six classes appear to rest on peripheral commentary. Classes appear to emerge from such things as the mood of community goodwill and speculation about population growth, new kinds of business, receding fears of the Depression, the expedience of mechanization, etc. As Robert

Lynd puts it, "The city's prevailing mood of optimism makes it view prosperity as normal while each recurrent setback tends to come as a surprise which local sentiment views as 'merely temporary' " (*Middletown in Transition* 13).

Indeed, even while Lynd acknowledges that the gap between manager and worker was greater in 1935 than in 1924, rather than interpret the gap as a deepening of a fundamental division between two classes, he broadens the band. He abandons the idea of a fundamental class structure in America at the same time that he recognizes a growing disparity in lives. He begins to blur distinctions between the two classes with the result that the individual, rather than the class, assumes primacy.

Lynd's own descriptions of the new classes evidence the disintegration. In the follow-up study, for example, low-class people are no longer described in terms of their livelihoods but in terms of "the ramshackle, unpainted cottages in the outlying unpaved streets of town" in which they lived. A third group, out of six, is described as those who would "never quite manage to be social peers of group two" (*Middletown in Transition* 458-60). These descriptions bear little resemblance to the earlier descriptions; they do possess a post-Depression coloration that tinges class description forever after. Lynd, in the face of Middletown's mythology and American ideology, caves in. The American society becomes one that, for all sociology could determine, possesses a multiplicity that defies classification. America is thus spared the reality of a hardened stratification, especially the stratification of job opportunities; instead, it can concentrate on variety, unmotivated orders, ambition.

But this revision of class structure did not have to happen. Other explanations of the changes in American work (and, as is most important to us, relationships to literacy) were possible. Frank Parkin, a British sociologist at the University of Kent, points this out. He calls such effusive sociology "pseudo-empirical," a "moral referendum" whose procedures work in the "way the Top Ten musical chart is constructed from the total selections of individual record buyers" (40). Parkin elaborates:

> To plot each person's position on a variety of different dimensions tends to produce statistical categories composed of those who have a similar "status profile," but it does not identify the type of social collectivities or classes which have

traditionally been the subject matter of stratification. Such
an approach tends to obscure the systematic nature of
inequality and the fact that it is grounded in the material
order in a fairly identifiable fashion. (17)

He concludes that testimonials often reveal the legitimation of
a set of criteria already "legitimized through society" (42). The
legitimation, of course, begins at the top to bring into concert
the beliefs and actions of those whose conformity to the current order is imperative. Thus, it is useful to recapitulate a
socially affirmed description of the classes that have enough
power to validate themselves.

The great result of the American sociological definition of
class is thus trivialization. Class cannot really be pinned down,
except in the ideal case, so it is in the end subjective and awe-
some. This is to return the sociological journey to the original
point of departure, the primacy and priority of the individual,
the unclassifiable human being. The structure that appears to
arrange individuals is basically epiphenomenal, contingent.
Mobility, or as sociologists put it, permeability, enervates
structures in such a manner that it is odd to think of a person
occupying or staying in a class. Sennett speaks of the pain of
leaving a class behind (139, 153) brought on by the almost
obligatory sense of the need to move up. John Dewey suggested
a compatible if rosier response to the mobility phenomenon. In
a society of bounty, he writes,

> if the culture pattern works out so that society is divided into
> two classes, the working group and the business (including
> professional) group, with two and a half times as many in the
> former as in the latter and with the chief ambition of the par-
> ents in the former class that their children should climb into
> the latter, that is doubtless because American life offers such
> unparalleled opportunities for each individual to prosper
> according to his virtues. . . . (10)

Class, in effect, is something like winning, and losers just do
not play well enough or have bad luck or, perhaps, never learn
the rules—out of stupidity, laziness, or because they come
from "inferior biological stock."

Awarding badges of superiority or inferiority, of course, is
not something an empirical sociology can do. "Superiority" is
a concept defined prior to the collection and bundling of human
features. The features may, in fact, distribute themselves, but

hierarchies emerge on the basis of other judgments. Asking informants to evaluate features may better reveal social indoctrination than objective evaluation. It certainly does not describe actual relations. Whence comes social agreement about lower class features, say, in an equal society? Of what use is the definition of lower class in a classless state?

Parkin, and others (Levitas 74–5), repudiate much American sociology on these grounds. Paraphrasing Karl Marx's assertion that the ruling ideas in a society are the ideas of the ruling class, Parkin says that

> it is plausible to regard social honor as an emergent property generated by the class system. More concisely, we can consider it as a system of social evaluation arising from the moral judgments of those who occupy dominant positions in the class structure. (41–42)

Or, to put it another way, classlessness does the bidding of class. Thus, American empirical sociology evolved within a definition of class, and its methodologies operate to keep it there. Because methodologies operate within social institutions, moreover, these institutions may be constrained to distort reality. Such is their social mandate. How, then, we might ask, can distortion be prevented or undone?

One way to address this question is to look at alternative conclusions to draw from the data we have already viewed. The Lynd study provides a valuable example.

In the follow-up study of Middletown, class did not have to be emulsified. The Lynds could have interpreted the splintering of Middletown and the cleaving to the myth of a classless society to be a conscious response to severe, increasingly entrenched, and verifiable divisions among lives of the Middletown citizens. Rather than supporting the emergence of more classes, the Lynd data could very well have supported the analysis of the ways in which class-divided citizens adapt to their society. For, in fact, the lines between adaptations were still drawn along economic realities. People spend the money they make within the economy they support. The leisure they engage in, the fabric of clothes they purchase, the security of their homes, and conditions of their streets provide descriptions, not prescriptions, of how people function along an economic continuum. The relationship of workers to work remained stable in Middletown in 1935; the artifacts of stability are what changed. Seen thus, the data provides a way to understand the internalization of domination under class society as well as the institutionalization of the social layout. Personal testimonials reveal structures rather than denigrate them, decry bundles of features rather than ratify them.

The example of the Lynds is important because the Lynds were seminal and wrong and because their work gives credence to a basis for continued exploitation rather than providing a rationale to examine and eradicate it. Certainly, as the Lynds suggest, the structures of American class possess peculiarly American characteristics. But the structures of American society are found inside daily life; they mediate the possibilities of American equality. What we still need to know, to reveal, is the nature of those structures. Certainly, the changing nature of work dictates how we must do this. At the same time, we need to discover ways to fashion trustworthy tools to interpret social information, not skew it.

One way is suggested by sociologist Frank Parkin. Parkin suggests that the way to view rifts in economic opportunity is to recognize within any society that citizens make their lives according to an economy; they live in commerce, not in isolation. Despite the sociomythology to the contrary, any life demands a social network, not rugged individualism. Both success and failure, lives of comfort and lives of misery, are social phenomena. This means that people who do not have enough to eat in a society in which there is enough food to go around are both hungry and socially demarcated. In a profit-driven economy, this instance is even more salient.

Marx worked out the idea fully. He claimed that the circumstances of equality begin in the circumstances of work; where a person stands in economic relation to what a person does to live determines the class of the person ("Wage Labor and Capital" 80). Those who stand in positions of employees, and who can see but cannot have the full worth of their own labor, stand in positions of exploitation. Thus, Marx said, "the proletariat [the working class] is recruited from all classes of the population" ("Manifesto" 42). Crudely, to be put in the position of reduced compensation is to be rendered into a class. (In this sense, ostensibly, no equation of money into labor ever achieves parity, which seems true enough.) An economy, in other words, bundles together peoples' lives, not dot-to-dot vanities. To understand the American class system, therefore, is to understand American work.

Thus, we have returned full circle. Class is a function of work. The question at this point is, once again, why English teachers should understand work. The answer is probably as difficult as any answer facing American education today. The answer is that work has changed, and the nature of the change is probably as complex and contingent as any change in history. The implication for English teachers is that the complexity impacts directly on their basic understanding of the nature of English, the purpose of English teaching, and the power of choice. Should English teachers wish to change English teaching, they will have to understand the interrelationships of English teaching to American work.

That they will be forced to do something along these lines is a sure thing. That is because the change in work is literacy. The change, in fact, is a change *in* literacy. That is why the English field is doubly involved, first as the harborer of traditional knowledge and second as the harbinger of turmoil.

It is safe to say that no one yet realizes the full extent of the change, perhaps because the change is neither complete nor evenly paced. Also, those who usually study such shifts have little experience with literacy as a concept. The overriding term for literacy in economic or labor studies is "information," and the terms by which information is discussed tend to describe it as a uniform, prepackaged product, much like any product that rolls off an assembly line. Because of this basic misconception (which was not conceived so differently in English or educational institutions even five years ago and still may not be differently conceived in many institutions today), analysts of radically different persuasions tend to wind up in similar and/or intractable positions. To understand as well as engage this dilemma, English teachers must be aware of contrasting assertions being made about the role of literacy in a changing economy. Good examples are provided by the work of Stanley Aronowitz and Daniel Bell.

Stanley Aronowitz, the author of *The Crisis in Historical Materialism: Class, Politics and Culture in Marxist Theory*, observes that "the old working class . . . has now all but passed into history in the United States" (83). What Aronowitz sees in the place of past history is a "third industrial revolution, now underway in the most technologically advanced countries [which] implies a transformation of the nature, but also of the character, of labor" (83).

Aronowitz is deeply disturbed by this transformation in the structural bases of American (or, better said, Western) labor. He is not alone. Other observers agree with Aronowitz's distrust of the changes in daily business procedures as well as adaptive behaviors in psychological relations. For example, Martin Oppenheimer believes that until recently high job esteem resided in "professionalism," an idea that he believes once implied:

> work involving discretion and judgment . . . work in which the worker produces an entire product, be it a painting, a surgical operation, a book, a bridge, or an idea; where the worker's pace, work place conditions, product, its use (and even to a degree its price) are largely determined by the worker. . . . (38)

Much work now, especially middle class work, is characterized by the deterioration of such factors. Professionalism has lost out to credentialism. Richard Sennett understands the loss to result in personal feelings of indignity, "an increase in men's feelings of meaninglessness in their actions" (259). Similarly, Dale Johnson and Christin O'Donnell describe the "dequalification" of middle class work as a collapse

> from relative independence to dependence, from superordination to subordination, from job security to underemployment in terms of education and skill level attained, and from economic well-being to relatively reduced levels of income. (230)

The overall reassessment of labor yields a state of deauthorized autonomy and supervised fragmentation.

Aronowitz catches the distinction between empowered and dequalified labor in a contrast between technologist and technician. A technician, he says, "performs rationalized labor whose nature is disguised by its limited supervisory function and responsibility, on the one hand, and the credentializing system that constitutes a prerequisite on the other" (*False Promises* 307). The result, Aronowitz says, is a "degradation" of the idea of skill as well as a change in the meaning of skill (*Crisis* 83) and a burial of the old scales that measured work; today, scales such as labor time neither measure current products of work nor select workers (*Crisis* 83). While Aronowitz and others distrust the change in work, a lack of documention of those changes complicates the issue even more.

A consequence of this lack is the variant use to which it can be put. Daniel Bell, the author of *The Coming of Post-Industrial Society*, also believes that the confusion about the change in the nature of work results from an inability to "define exactly what is changing" (42). However, Bell, unlike Aronowitz, is excited by the prospects of change. Bell believes that an information society is consonant with the establishment of a "meritocracy."

This set of circumstances is ideal for Bell. According to Bell, people will get knowledge by getting educated. Those who get educated best will be those who get the most knowledge and who can handle it most cleverly and efficiently. Those folks will be the successful individuals and will sit at the top of the social heap. The heap, however, will itself smarten up; if education does its job, society will become a meritocracy, which education already is (or should be). As he says,

> Questions of inequality have little to do with the issue of meritocracy—if we define a meritocracy as those who have earned status or have achieved authority by competence. (27)

On this basis, therefore, unsuccessful or unclever people get what they deserve. Bell is fully committed to the idea that American society will need "an intelligentsia" who can handle concepts and a whole other group who can handle data (43). The remedy for those whose lives and livelihoods are dispossessed by science and technology is also clear: they must repossess, retrain, retool, reskill themselves in the knowledge of science and technology—the stuff of the American dream. In this way, of course, within the Bell scenario, knowledge does not merely preserve the status quo; it creates it and effectively explains the underclass remarked by Aronowitz and Kopkind. People who do not avail themselves of the new knowledge are the people who drop out, or down, as the case may be, to the levels of the under- and unemployed. The important idea at stake is how literacy informs labor. The definition of labor prior to its change in the information economy is shared at the outset by Aronowitz and Bell.

The preinformation economy, both would agree, identifies workers' positions in the economy mostly according to profit quotas. People who spun cotton thread in textile mills, for example, produced profit in terms of the volume of cotton they used, the time they spent at their machines, the hourly wages they drew. Managers, on the other hand, produced profit by managing the relationships between workers, hours, and machines. The amount of money spent on producing cloth had to be exceeded by the amount of money obtained through its distribution and purchase. Efforts to increase the gap characterize American business.

But what happens when production, distribution, and purchase of material goods become dependent on information—the production, distribution, and purchase of literacy? To the minds of recent labor economists such as Aronowitz and Bell, information reorganizes the calculation. Not only does an information age bring with it robots who replace weavers and spinners (or who at least drastically reduce their numbers), but it changes all the relationships. People and words present new relationships since, to put it crudely, profit quotas cannot be hung directly on word output. Creativity—what can be done with information—complicates the scene even more. Where there was always the need to manage other people's output, as well as one's own, managing information requires wholesale reconsideration of ideas such as time, output, logic.

Thus, Bell and Aronowitz share a perspective on the source of economic change. The crux of the matter is whether or not they share the same ideas about information. The conundrum is that they do.

Bell nails information to output. Information, for him, is an interchangeable notion with knowledge, knowledge an interchangeable notion with science and technology. Bell's definition of knowledge expressly avoids the fields of "news and entertainment" to center on mechanistic, quantifiable scientific data; in his words, knowledge is

> a set of organized statements of acts or ideas, presenting a reasoned judgment or an experimental result, which is transmitted to others through some communication medium in some systematic form. (175)

Knowledge underwrites science and technology, which underwrite information. It possesses a mystique that in turn is possessed by "those in knowledge production"—according to Aronowitz (*Crisis* 81). Others revere knowledge so much as to discard the term. Jeremy Campbell, in *Grammatical Man: Information, Entropy, Language, and Life*, claims that to the "powerful theories of chemistry and physics [science and technology] must be added a late arrival: a theory of information. Nature must be interpreted as matter, energy, and information" (16). Business analysts, as market and general-appeal publications attest, can hardly contain the possibilities for information systems that store not just information but other systems of storage as well.

Aronowitz also believes that mechanisms of information hook into mechanisms of work. He is concerned to account for the disappearance of certain classes within the transforming system of Western free enterprise, a system that he knows neither loses nor equalizes members of these classes but shoves them aside. The focus on where people go sometimes obscures his realization that knowledge—information, literacy—is the fulcrum of the shift, but the realization is there. For example, he says that other (notably Marxist) economic theories have simply failed to account for the impact of information on the status of workers:

> Marxism has not only been unable to theorize the role of the "middle strata" in modern capitalism in a manner appropriate to changes in *the relation of knowledge to the production or to the question entailed by the advent of consumer society,* it has also been unable to theorize the formation of the new underclass in advanced capitalist societies. [emphasis added] (*Crisis* 90)

Thus, Aronowitz expresses awareness of and bafflement by the engine that moves marginalization not merely upward and downward but laterally in an information society. As Andrew Kopkind puts it, in the emerging American economy "service managers, franchise workers, and venture capitalists" sit "on a huge underclass of burger wrappers and security guards" (451). The venture capitalist of today counts among his assets his access to knowledge; burger wrappers are the information poor. These poor may not be the usual poor, however. They may be entirely new groups of people. Michael Harrington in an updated "Afterword" to *The Other America* identifies a population of between seven and nineteen million people who ostensibly choose not to re-educate themselves and to remain unemployed and impoverished; their numbers appear to be required by "normal" free enterprise (214).

The explanation for the disparity between Aronowitz's and Bell's understanding is a static notion of literacy. For both Aronowitz and Bell, information or knowledge or literacy is *stuff,* a *body* of information. Literacy is a *thing* that assumes two forms. First, it is digital. Second, it is acquired via command and demand. It works in channels, input-output. Input comes from the top, the outside. Output comes from the bottom. As with any machine, the raw material is machined, and the product is sold. The transfer is essentially passive. This overstates Aronowitz's position, but not much. When he and Henry Giroux blame much of the literacy crisis on overcrowded classrooms, lack of books, and weary administrators and teachers (Aronowitz and Giroux 64), they essentially fall into the knowledge-out-there, input-output syndrome. For both Bell and Aronowitz, therefore, asking for and receiving knowledge are different sides of the same coin: a person who wants knowledge—who wants to work—is a person who gets it.

Reinventing one's livelihood is tough, Aronowitz and Kopkind would no doubt agree. But it is equally tough to overlook the peculiar phenomenon of mass self-destruction. Why would so many people choose to disqualify themselves from the possibilities of labor? Equally odd, why do such great numbers of people choose to attain a minimum kind of knowledge that puts them in positions, as Aronowitz says, "of social labor that is fragmented, degraded, and stratified, just like the private corporate sector" (*Crisis* 183). In the face of the promise of "equal information," are we to assume that large groups of people watch passively as their economic security, psychological well-being, and standards of living erode? The answer must be no.

Science and technology and the information revolution they breed are not forms of liberation but another form of domination. Science and technology merely disguise "factory-like" conditions in technical, even "upscale" professions. This according to Aronowitz (*False Promises* 294). The issue, therefore, for Aronowitz and Bell and for us is not how "technical" information gives access to greater freedom and opportunity but how it takes it away.

Aronowitz knows that the blue-collar/white-collar division no longer describes class divisions: "It is a category of social ideology rather than of social science" (*False Promises* 294). Stereotypical white-collar office situations, for example, have deteriorated (especially for women) into rooms of "deafening" keypunch noise; and whereas secretaries and bosses may lunch together (echoes of Warner) they do not share class (*False Promises* 291–292).

Bell's scenario, on the other hand, welcomes ambiguity in class divisions; increasing numbers of divisions, indeed, negate a class society (echoes, again, of Warner and the Lynds).

Information is free to be had, it is ubiquitous, it is endless. The only issue for Bell is how the commodity, this knowledge, is to be distributed. For Aronowitz, who believes, too, that "knowledge has become the main productive force" (*Crisis* 83), the dilemma is similar. "To combat . . . inequality," he and Giroux say, "students require knowledge (of which skills are derivative) and, most of all, hope in their collective powers to change the world . . . " (66). Class is a matter of "exclusion from the mainstream of economic life" (*False Promises* 11); today, he could easily substitute "knowledge" for "economic life," for knowledge is access, and certain kinds of knowledge are premium.

Bell and Aronowitz agree on the sources of socioeconomic transformation. The upshot of this transformation is clear. Class stays the same. Or, more to the point, class becomes what it has always been, an unfair system of ownership.

It is possible that a system of ownership built on the ownership of literacy is more violent than past systems, however. Though it seems difficult to surpass the violence of systems of indenture, slavery, industrialism, and the exploitation of immigrant or migrant labor, literacy provides a unique bottleneck. Unlike a gun, whose least precedent is literacy, literacy legitimates itself. To be literate is to be legitimate; not to be literate is to beg the question. The question is whether or not literacy possesses powers unlike other technologies. The only way to address the question is to be literate. What more effective form of abuse than to offer clandestine services.

Bell and Aronowitz would not find themselves riveted to the power of literacy if they did not share a definition of literacy. But if knowledge is not a thing but an act, and people learn not by being but by acting, then the status of knowledge depends on the status of the actors. Knowledge is not necessarily linguistic; some acts do not require words. Furthermore, knowledge assumes historical acting; history comes to be made and remade and varies in its interpretation as societies vary in their upkeep. The opportunities to know depend on the relationships people maintain, the types of opportunities they have to gain access to sources of knowledge, the culture and experiences they bring to learning, and the sanctions or measures that govern possible consequences.

The interchanges so described represent complex situations that have not been examined carefully in studies of literacy and class structure. The following chapters are an attempt to open such an examination by looking at how we look at literacy, the theories about literacy we weave, and the ways we presume to program literacy into the lives of social groups and the people who make them up. As a starting point, we might ask how the American system of work might respond to a contextual theory of knowledge. Since knowledge within a free economy is useful in accordance with the needs and aims of private profit, then the way to control knowledge is to regulate access and rigidify function—to co-opt the context, in other words.

The American society is a literate society in which oral language communication lacks literacy's rubber stamp. Valid communication is written text. Valid uses of communication—i.e., profitable, legalized ones—require literacy. Today, the link between decisions about capital and decisions about social, economic intercourse is literacy. Literacy is the language of profit; in America, profit begs text. As Aronowitz says, "reading and writing are conditions of survival . . . " ("Toward Redefining Literacy" 54). Literacy is, if nothing else, the condition of postindustrialism. A worker's possibilities are contained by his ability to negotiate subjects of capital. In contemporary capitalism in the United States, then, literacy and class are fused. Thus, both are being reorganized.

At the same time that literacy is an economic and social regulation, it is also taught. The functional issue of how literacy comes to distribute class relations involves the ways of teaching. Theories and pedagogies of literacy set the parameters for interchange. Acquisition becomes the mediator of social relations; teaching, the arbiter. This is to say that literacy is a function of culture, social experience, and sanction. Literacy education begins in the ideas of the socially and economically dominant class and it takes the forms of socially acceptable subjects, stylistically permissible forms, ranges of difference or deviance, baselines of gratification. Becoming literate signifies in large part the ability to conform or, at least, to appear conformist. The teaching of literacy, in turn, is a regulation of access.

For example, a tactic of computer advertising in the United States is to warn parents that without home-computerized instruction, children will not get ahead in school. Actually, the computer may only serve as an indicator of the advantages already bestowed by a student's class. The book in early eighteenth-century England assumed a similar status. Almost any book cost ten times what a laborer made in a week, if not more (Watt 41). The use of the book, though purportedly to educate the buying family, merely identified the class of the buyer, not the merit of the book or, contrary to popular belief, the illiteracy of the nonbuyer. The computer, or the book, indexes social class, not conditions of knowledge. This distinction is one the confusion of which is promulgated by the contemporary idealism of literacy. Thus, the concept of literacy that animates Bell and stymies Aronowitz boils down to daily realities and translates rather than transforms labor relations. New knowledge promises new opportunity, but no new equality appears imminent. Bell, of course, supposes that many people have as yet chosen to avail themselves of the knowledge extant. Aronowitz cannot support such an explanation.

In the past, when class was supposedly easier to see (racial structures, as well), it always worked out predictably that children of mill life or children of segregation did not learn to read and write very well (a lie, of course) and so went to their natural calling. On the other hand, children who did become standardized literates were naturally called to desks. Others did not get as far as having the option. Now that class is obscured, and many who were always presumed to be in the protected classes are losing that protection, the mechanism for distribution appears to fall into question. A reassessment of that mechanism, however, might reveal less a disintegration of class lines than a retrenchment along those lines, so that socioeconomic opportunities that different groups of students might find and do and look forward to may change but the groups themselves shift only slightly. As the margins grow wider, of course, the freedoms grow narrower. How this happens, relevant to an axis of literacy, presents an interesting question.

Where it happens, of course, is in school. It is to institutionalized American education, therefore, that the argument turns next.

CHAPTER TWO

IDEOLOGIES OF LITERACY

◆

The ways in which literacy is thought about in this country are reductive and dangerous. In their application, they narrow the range of pedagogy and suppress the possibilities of research. This is the real literacy crisis. The purpose of this chapter is to understand how an often silent but powerful ideology operates within the structures of American literacy.

To understand the ideology of literacy requires us to do two things. The first is to wrestle with the idea of ideology. Unfortunately, ideology is a term that brings with it a lot of baggage, arguably more baggage than many specialized terms. It is a term that often polarizes discussions among groups of educators, English educators being no exception. Yet to come to grips with the term is necessary if we are to understand why it enters some conversations and not others and, more important, why it is divisive. The second thing to do is to carry an understanding of ideology into an understanding of literacy. The caveat is that this study, too, is governed by an ideology. We in English departments usually believe that what we are doing is right. We believe this in spite of the fact that we often feel we do not get the right results. At the same time, many of us have rarely

21

examined why we think we are right. This chapter challenges the notion of our rightness.

Perhaps the most neutral way to speak of an ideology is as a "system of ideas" (Poulantzas 17). The emphasis is on "system." Ideas in an ideology conform to one another. This is not to say that the "fit" among ideas is perfect, or even that we can determine specific matchups (a situation Louis Althusser calls "overdetermined") but usually contradictions resolve in a "greater" vision. The "greater" vision, in fact, is the ideology.

Max Weber insists upon the necessity of ideologies but he refuses to adopt a party line. In *The Methodology of the Social Sciences* he describes how there can be no selection or interpretation of data without reference to "evaluative ideas," ideas that are not themselves deducible from the data. Indeed, for Weber, the opposite is true. He says, "The 'objectivity' of the social sciences depends rather on the fact that the empirical data is derived from these evaluative ideas" (111). This is no small point. Weber means that people see things according to rules that they may not see. People may see what they think they must, what they have always seen. This circumstance skews vision, perhaps all vision.

A more highly politicized definition of ideology is supplied by Terry Eagleton, a Marxist literary theorist. Eagleton's focus is on the destructiveness of ideology. Eagleton is difficult to read, but he nails the power of ideology to mispresent itself. Ideology, he says, is

> a relatively coherent set of "discourses" of values, representations and beliefs which [are] realized in certain material apparatuses and related to the structures of material production so to reflect the experiential relations of individual subjects to their social conditions as to guarantee those misperceptions of the "real" which contribute to the reproduction of the dominant social relations. (54)

Eagleton targets the grave danger of ideologies: they tend to subsume ideas according to powerful interests. They tend to make people with limited power feel powerful.

Ideology in literacy does not prove an exception to the rule. First, many researchers appear ignorant or arrogant of the ideological frameworks in which they work. They would like, as Eagleton says of historical materialists, to be allowed to step "outside the terrain of competing 'long perspectives' in order to theorize the conditions of their possibility" (16). This view,

Eagleton observes, is a convenient but questionable view. More seriously, some researchers seem unable or unwilling to view the frustration of their work as ideologically intolerable; thus, they shape their work to fit the ideology. Eagleton requires more than this. He concludes,

> the moment when a material or intellectual practice begins to "think itself," to take itself as an object of intellectual inquiry, is clearly of dominant significance in the development of that practice; it will certainly never be the same again. (17)

The practice of researching literacy and the uses we reassert or invent for it have changed their object just as they have changed one another.

One of the clearest ideological issues we must finally address is the impetus for such change. To do so, we will look at several studies, studies that focus either directly on literacy or on literacy within the framework of educational models of comprehension.

The issue of literacy to the extent that it supersedes most other educational issues entered the national consciousness in the early 1970s. To date, the most prescient American study of the meaning of literacy was published in 1981. *The Psychology of Literacy* by Sylvia Scribner and Michael Cole consists of a multifaceted investigation of the Vai people of Liberia. The investigation has had great impact, not the least for its correlative ability to articulate central Western beliefs about the effects of literacy. Its shift toward a culture-relative understanding of literacy is a second appeal. Another aspect of the study, however, renders the investigation most interesting for our purposes, and that is the curious duality of the conclusions. As the present analysis will argue, it is this duality, often consisting of direct contradiction, that proves most instructive and most ideological.

Within Scribner and Cole's study, the implications for a complete revision of thinking about literacy are in open evidence. They begin in, and are beholden to, several features: a rigorous, interdisciplinary method, clear enunciation of the original questions, and acknowledgment of the difficulties the conceptual nuances pose. To ensure as much accuracy and integrity as possible in gathering data, Scribner and Cole combine the usual testing/experimental plans of cognitive psychology (using "instruments" such as Forced-Choice Longest-Word tests, for example) with interviews, question-naires, and ethnographic observation "in the hope that each [method] might check and supplement the other" (22). They do so in recognition of the "covariation of literacy" with all aspects of social life, aspects that present "a formidable obsta-cle to research on educational effects, and a point to which we will constantly return" (10). The tight weave among social strands of "educational" life is precisely what Scribner and Cole would like to loosen in order to inspect. Theirs, too, is the longstanding hypothesis "that literacy introduces a great divide among human societies" (4), but their interest is to dis-tinguish the features that might exist alongside this divide. The overall question is formulated thus: "Is literacy a surrogate for schooling?" (20) If it is or is not, they hope to be able to charac-terize the separatism, to

> demonstrate an association between antecedent literacy prac-tices and consequent cognitive performance, and to do so under analytic conditions that would clearly establish liter-acy as a causal factor. (18)

The priority emphasis on cognition, of course, may itself ham-per more than aid the progress, but the probability for demarca-tion among kinds of effects (skills)—cognitive versus social versus types of cognicity—appears greater in the Vai society than in most. This is why Scribner and Cole chose the Vai, who present a special setting that suggests a natural separation between schooling and literacy and also affords the opportunity to measure or evaluate the consequence of each "cause." As Scribner and Cole put it,

> We were drawn to Vai society in the first place because we hoped that the existence of an indigenous script, transmitted outside of an institutional setting and having no connection with Western-type school, would make it possible to disen-tangle literacy effects from school effects. (19)

They presumed to capitalize, in effect, on a unique laboratory-type situation that could inform Western institutions as to the extricability of the functions of education.

The study Scribner and Cole conducted was broad and thor-ough. The researchers did not shy away from tough questions; they addressed issues of metalinguistic ability as well as variation in direction-giving expertise, for example, among Vai literates, nonliterates, and schooled biliterates. At almost every turn, Scribner and Cole took care to examine the purposes of their tests and, as they report, more than once changed the direction of research. So, it is momentous when, at the end of the process, they announce a dearth of results. In their words, "If we were to regard only general consequences as worthy of serious attention, we would have to dismiss the literacy activities among the Vai as being of little psychological interest" (324). At a later point, they conclude a discussion of correlations between unschooled Vai literacy and general ability tasks with an equally hapless response:

> Vai script literacy was associated with modest contributions on three general ability tasks: experts who taught the script showed a preference for form or number in sorting geometric figures; Vai script reading score contributed to performance on story recall and language objectivity tasks in one of their administrations; Vai script letter writing was associated with more categorical choices of food items. We have no principled explanations of these spotty effects. (344)

To be sure, Scribner and Cole found more logical effects associated with Vai script literacy when it was associated with other literacies and school. Vai script literates could use "graphic symbols to represent language" and use "language as a means of instruction" in discussion of, say, grammar or board-game rules (254). Vai literates, in other words, could talk about Vai script in ways that Vai nonliterates could not.

However, Scribner and Cole found that nonliterates performed as well as or better than literates on many tasks, even those specific to literacy technology: "Even on tasks closely related to script activities, such as reading or writing with pictures, some nonliterates did as well as those with school or literacy experience" (251). Scribner and Cole could only conclude that "literacy promotes skills among the Vai but we cannot and do not claim that literacy is a necessary and sufficient condition for any of the skills we assessed" (251). The assertion is remarkable for a study that set out to discover the effects of an "antecedent" literacy.

In one sense, Scribner and Cole's book should end here. That it does not is partly attributable to its originality—no one had tried to examine literacy in these ways before. Vai culture suggests to Scribner and Cole, however, that literacy means something else, so they continue the study in search of that. They propose that literacy is always bound up with a practice. The idea of practice, they say,

> guides the way we seek to understand literacy. Instead of focusing exclusively on the technology of a writing system and its reputed consequences . . . we approach literacy as a set of organized practices which make use of a symbol system and a technology for producing it. . . . The nature of these practices, including, of course, their technological aspects, will determine the kinds of skills [consequences] associated with literacy. (236)

In a more strongly worded and potentially explosive statement, they assert that "inquiries into the cognitive consequences of literacy are *inquiries into the impact of socially organized practices in other domains*" (237; emphasis added). They disclaim, thereby, the notion of an insular literacy. Literacy amounts to a technology whose nature is always social, or, at least, always socially derived and socially defined. This exigence, moreover, is specific and rooted:

> In order to identify the consequences of literacy, we need to consider the specific characteristics of specific practices. And, in order to conduct such an analysis, we need to understand the larger social system that generates certain kinds of practices (and not others). (237)

In other words, literacy may be cognitively superfluous; its cognitive effects, at best, are "spotty" and unexplainable.

The question that arises haunts all research into literacy. Are there *any* effects of literacy or are all effects in which literacy is involved *other* effects? Scribner and Cole ask this rhetorically:

> Can we bring our evidence of localized and specific changes [attributed to literacy] into relation with scholars' grand speculations about literacy and thought? Or is there no meeting ground between the two sets of terms? (234)

Though recondite, an answer is not impossible within the data Scribner and Cole have amassed. To pursue it, however, requires something very much like stopping in one's tracks upon the sudden realization that the paths have been circular. If literacy is not an explanatory principle for a practice, then what explains literacy? What is the practice of a society that practices literacy, and what, then, would literacy mean? These certainly are the kinds of questions to be mulled over. The answers, indeed, may force a complete reevaluation of the undertaking, in this case a reevaluation of the focus of the study. This is a very hard thing for researchers to do. Unfortunately, faced with these questions, Scribner and Cole do the expected thing. They retreat.

When it seemed clear that literacy could not be found to produce much of anything useful, Scribner and Cole tried to expand their field of investigation. They did not abandon their awe of literacy:

> [We] were unwilling to abandon the possibility that there might be some form of pervasive intellectual changes related to literacy per se. Turning away from developmental theorizing about higher-order thinking and memory skills, we decided to examine cognitive change in domains more closely related to acquisition and use of written language. (134)

In certain respects, Scribner and Cole's tenacity is admirable. Their retrenchment, however, promises little. They already know that the results of literacy-specific testing are unclear and narrow. Yet they force a conclusion unsupported by their own study: "However modest and specialized the outcomes, our studies among the Vai provide the first direct evidence that literacy makes some difference to some skills in some contexts" (234). The equivocation of "some difference" is a smokescreen Scribner and Cole send up again and again. Our question must be this: What explains the choice to affirm a hypothesis that does not pan out?

One source of constraint can be seen in a curious statement that excuses the study for failing to take its own advice; it occurs just after Scribner and Cole have pronounced the unique, if odd, effects of literacy. They say:

> To give a satisfactory account of the nature and significances of the differences [between literacies and nonliteracies] we found—and failed to find—we would need to draw on some well specified theory of cognition, especially a theory spelling out the mechanism by which social factors affect cognitive variation. No such theory was at hand when we commenced our work, and none is at hand today to help us interpret it. (234)

Scribner and Cole must be speaking in terms of theories within their own field; they must require, and be limited by, a social theory generated by cognitive psychology, which would be a very strange thing, indeed. They themselves confirm this limitation. In an appendix to the study, they evidence awareness of the historical origin and significance of Vai script. They observe that it possesses the function of keeping "business" within the community secret from those outside; they notice that Vai script appears at the approximate time of nineteenth-century imperialism in Africa. They hypothesize that the social stratification of script literacy is tied to the agricultural economy. They even surmise an "ideological value" of script "in traditional activities, pragmatic values in trade, and political values ... in a region beset by local colonization and foreign penetration" (269). Yet, they say, "no direct evidence supports [our] speculation," and they defer to the speculations of others to explain the life of the script (269). They reduce what they cannot explain to the inexplicable.

This observation is less a criticism of Scribner and Cole than it is a lament over the confines of traditional academic disciplines. In retrospect, it is easy to see how the assumptions and traditions of one discipline come to dominate an entire undertaking, even those aspects that seemed extradisciplinary. Scribner and Cole import a psychology of cognition to keep interpretations of literacy within a cognitive framework. This is ideology. Unfortunately, cognition is not itself an arbitrary fact. It, too, comes out of a social matrix and is interwoven with the social life that cognizes, or evaluates, effects. The notion that a society can be divvied up according to its cognitive performances diminishes the importance of society while it elevates individual psychology. In Scribner and Cole's study, the content of the Vai society does not materialize. The Vai have already been taxonomized before the Vai are met. This neglect of society suggests precisely the questions to raise about Scribner and Cole and many other literacy researchers: What is the researchers' culture? What are their assumptions? On what economic and material bases do they live? Indeed, from what kind of society does such a taxonomy come and of what use is it to the society to make separable and separate ideas and kinds of literacy, cognition, and social relationship or effects?

An explanation entails a reexamination of the meaning of literacy in Western society, a meaning that is so central to be tacit and so tacit to be manipulative. That meaning is shot through with Western assumptions of what societies do and how societies organize their relationships. Underlying the assumptions is the tacit understanding that people can be understood in terms of their uses and that literacy, in particular, can be understood in terms of its ends. This underlying assumption, as antisocial as it may be in the Vai society, runs throughout the commentary on that society. We can analyze how this assumption operates in two ways.

The first, on the surface, may appear illogical, even unfair. It is the reliance of the research on the *artifact* of literacy to identify a literate occasion, an occasion in which speculation about literacy can go on. Scribner and Cole go to Vai country to extrapolate from Vai script, and it is Vai script literacy they invoke to discover pure cognitive effects of a pure, unschooled technology. The Vai print is the Vai literacy, in other words; wherever there is print, there is literacy. Scribner and Cole seem to know the pitfalls of this simplistic attitude, this equation of the artifact with the literacy. "A piece of writing," they say, "whatever its form, serves as a flag to signal activities in the ongoing stream of behavior that *may have some component skills in common*" (258; emphasis added). Yet rather than proceed in the direction this statement would indicate, to unearth the origin and dictates of these skills, Scribner and Cole close ranks and emphasize again, the specific cognitive features attached to discrete literate occasions. Thus, the thingness of the literacy is preserved, even if thingness is converted into a conceptual idea. In fact, such a conversion reembeds literacy within the psychological discipline of Scribner and Cole—literacy becomes a cognitive structure as it meets psychological criteria for cognition.

One of those criteria is that cognition be quantifiable. As a result, Scribner and Cole seem at times to be caught up in shooting at anything that moves in the literacy wilderness. Every time they see print, they see another target. Another result is that the effects of literacy are "Western" reproductions of Scribner and Cole's own society. These are the effects they cannot find, much less quantify. They say,

> Vai literacy is not a vehicle for introducing new ways of life. We have called it literacy without education because it does not open doors to vicarious experience, new bodies of knowledge, or new ways of thinking about major life problems. (238)

The assumptions here are striking.

Is this what literacy is supposed to do—introduce vicariousness, import new information or problem-solving techniques, please, or instruct? If literacy does not do this, does it fail to educate? Educate about what? Surely, the only possible reply is educate in Western ways, ways of vicarious experience and knowledge gathering explicitly linked to literacy. Scribner and Cole can think of "no educational activity that is mediated by standardized written material in Vai script" (238). More specifically, and dramatically for us, they are perplexed that for the Vai, literacy is not a tool that enables one person to dominate another. They are perplexed to find that

> those who do not know [the Vai script literacy] get along quite well. We see no evidence that they are barred from leadership roles in the social system or from traditional occupations because they cannot read and write. Vai script literacy is not essential either to maintain or to elaborate customary ways of life. (238)

But why should literacy bring hardship? The society of Scribner and Cole, not the society of the Vai, is the one that stakes much on the oppressive powers of literacy. In Vai society, something goes on that looks like literacy, but it does not deliver the way Western literacy does.

Scribner and Cole, like the Lynds before them, could have reconsidered their observations. Other lenses might interpret the Vai data in terms less impeded by Western ideology. As Scribner and Cole acknowledge, the Vai script has a history. Every time the literacy flag goes up, we can assume history must also be involved. A broad observation might be that Vai script, given the anticolonialism of its origin, came into existence to ward off the imperialism or exploitation of foreign colonists. As Scribner and Cole note, Vai literacy instruction takes place almost invariably one-on-one, between older males, and outside of institutions. (Apparently, gender separation in Vai society *is* like that in most other societies, another argument for the social co-option of literacy.) There are no "standardized" texts. Reading and writing are "inextricably" linked (67). The apparent elusiveness of Vai literacy may well be an assertion of (male) independence. At the same time, Scribner and Cole discern that Vai literacy "has not set off dramatic modernizing sequences" or "become a mass literacy" (238). We might ask, however, if it ever would have. If in the beginning Vai literacy hid familiar Vai interests (and economics) from colonialists, it might not continue to do so, given the "success" of colonialism. Vai literacy, in other words, may continue to operate but without original results. Meanwhile, for the Vai to learn English literacy is to opt out or, more likely, be forced out, of Vai society. Why then has Vai literacy persisted?

One would surmise a primary reason to be solidarity. Another might be social discontinuity or confusion, or, in fact, despair. Vai literacy to the Vai may be an allusion to the past, to a juncture where independence met domination to the extent that memories of independence both solidify and recall social demise. Scribner and Cole, for example, note that the birth mortality rate in Liberia is 50 percent; a number of the Vai script letters that circulate concern what Scribner and Cole call "ubiquitous" funerals. Vai life, in other words, is the subject of Vai literacy; the use is Western only as the saddest barometer of Western influence. The sad realization is, if this study is any indication, that the West could care less.

To the extent that original reasons for analyzing Scribner and Cole were to appreciate their findings about literacy and to observe the discords of research and reporting, this analysis has swung full circle. What, we ask now, can we conclude from a vast study on literacy that comes up blank and cannot say it, that generates fascinating data but cannot process it? We can certainly conclude that the business of literacy research is pressed for answers. We can also conclude that literacy researchers have a vested interest in finding certain kinds of results. To say of the Vai that literacy has no effects is tantamount in the West to saying that there is no literacy. That, however, constitutes an unacceptable conclusion. The full equation—no effects, no literacy, no society—deconstructs the entire enterprise.

Scribner and Cole, of course, are not the only researchers constrained by ideologies of literacy. In this respect, it is useful to turn to a "purely" American study, *Adult Illiteracy in the United States: A Report to the Ford Foundation* by Carman St. John Hunter and David Harman. Like *The Psychology of Literacy*, this report experiences similar divisions of methodology and practice and fails also to see the basis of the schism. Hunter and Harman, too, are haunted by dualities sprung from the need to privatize literacy as well as root it in the society. A pragmatic difference between their report and Scribner and Cole's is that Hunter and Harman are in positions to recommend programs for the amelioration of the American society.

Yet their recommendations further a legacy of oscillation contained along a vertical rather than lateral conception of social action.

The first step Hunter and Harman take is to divide literacy in half, into something they call conventional (almost neighborhood-specific) and functional literacy. The definition of functional literacy concerns us most as it is the definition ostensibly open to generalized address. Functional literacy constitutes

> the possession of skills perceived as necessary by particular persons and groups to fulfill their own self-determined objectives as family and community members, citizens, consumers, job-holders, and members of social, religious, or other associations of their choosing. (17)

As broad and egalitarian as this definition may appear, implicit within it are the familiar contradictions. These contradictions are between literacy and society and also between individuals in their groups and the larger society. Literacy is a "particular" skill to be deployed to meet a person's own "self-determined objectives." The location of self-determination among the various communal agencies diffuses to some extent the secularization of literacy, but this listing also works to obscure. Is it the case, for example, that literacy within the family operates on the same grounds that it does in the church or on the job? Are we to assume that the idea of family is uniform? That this report makes these assumptions rather than bringing them into question is ideological. This is made quite clear when Hunter and Harman speak of the "unlettered" in foreign countries who

> when given an opportunity to define their own needs . . . are likely to stress first their economic problems, followed by such personal concerns as family living, child care, health, and nutrition. (8)

The authors add, "What bearing, if any, does this have on adult life in the United States?" (8)

What bearing indeed unless the needs of literacy are also the needs of economic survival. The categorical move to separate needs from one another—from money, from "personal" habits, from "community" life—is just another symptom of the rigid separation of the idea of literacy from the dictates of its use.

Hunter and Harman's separation has its cognitive dimensions, also. Illiterates, for example, divide into subgroups who differ not only in ethnicity and race and culture and well-being but "they differ in their present levels of knowledge, how they process information, their motives for learning, their consciousness of community identity, and how they interact with the larger surrounding society" (104). One wonders if the peculiarities of subgroup cognicity will ever test favorably on traditional social measurements.

The conclusion of Hunter and Harman's report on illiteracy thus presents a frustrating situation. The authors could hardly be more forthright: "We support programs that increase the skills of community members to interact with and change the mainstream culture and its institutions" (105). But while they endorse empowerment and change, they contain them within the society that secures the opposite. One wonders, in other words, about the will or abilities of social agencies such as the Ford Foundation, which supported Hunter and Harman's work, to ally with illiterate subgroups to change "mainstream culture." Mainstream culture secures the studies that it begets.

The study of the Vai and the study of illiterates in America elaborate each other. From the more abstract realms of Western ideology brought to bear on undeveloped economies, the working out of the forms and content of ideological presuppositions within the lives of real Westerners takes on familiar appearances. Scribner and Cole just barely suggest a radical devaluation of literacy; their failure to follow their own argument to its conclusions mirrors the American practice of mission literacy and the faith that there simply must be some good that comes from what we all know to be good.

The unwillingness to either relinquish or expand notions of literacy is riveted in American economic and educational structures. At the same time, the current interest in literacy departs from a fund of traditional and nontraditional sources. Few of the present advocates, however, escape the silent mandate to keep the status quo where it is. The first advocacy group is the most traditional, its interests most vested and, up until now, most protected. This is the group of English teachers and the teachers of English teachers. The question of their ideological co-option is so apparent as to be self-explanatory, but this group is powerful and prolific, and so its work needs examination for what it is.

The second group, and "group" in this case is a loose term, consists of researchers who come from the domains of Scribner and Cole and allied social-science disciplines; these are field psychologists, sociologists, sociolinguists who take their methodological cue from social anthropology. The current popularity and increasing power of this group deserves close attention as does the social scientist's tendency to institute wholesale empirical epistemologies about the nature and validity of "observation" while failing to scrutinize the processes they advocate.

The third group is the smallest and espouses the only critique of the literacy flurry. In America, Henry Giroux, and Michael Holzman and Marilyn Cooper are the most prolific writers out of this perspective, although they are preceded by people like James Sledd and Linda Finlay, scholars who write less than they practice their beliefs. There is a much larger group of British theorists who deal specifically with issues of literacy; they are Peter Medway and Mike Torbe, Harold Rosen, Margaret Meek, James Britton, Nancy Martin, and Brian Street. The American inability to escape certain embedded traditions of literacy is highly instructive about the difficulty American education faces.

In the first group, there are numerous examples of the entrenched response to the need to research and to understand literacy. These efforts might be most kindly termed provincial. An early 1980s collection of essays published by the Modern Language Association (prior to the splintering of some members of the organization into a small but vociferous literacy faction) is typical. Despite its contemporariness, *Literacy for Life*, 1983, edited by Richard Bailey and Robin Fosheim, is a genuine source of traditional views. For example, in it Edwin J. Delattre in an essay titled "The Insiders" differentiates between the insiders, American literates, and the outsiders, American illiterates. It has come to Delattre's attention that

> many outsiders do not even know they are outsiders; they think the world is for everyone as it is for them. The challenge for teachers . . . is to draw outsiders far enough inside to detect the difference. Learners must have the chance to know

> with brilliant clarity what it feels like to be outsiders and to
> know they are outside. (53)

The failure of Delattre to question the content of the inside is
rivaled only by his belief that students who fail to become
acceptably literate have no idea of the benefits or constraints of
literacy or of the motives of those who would keep students
illiterate. Delattre is not singular, however. The idea of wel-
come is widespread; advertising and extending invitations into
literacy clubs and communities range across the language/
humanities disciplines from developmental specialties (Smith,
Essays) to the domains of postmodernist literary criticism
(Fish). It is as though all one has to do is to invite the illiterate
to dinner.

However, the philosophical tenor of English scholars is less
concentrated on broad statements of generosity than it is fragmented into lists of questions addressed to specifics. Literacy is
not merely a separate issue but a startling one. "What is literacy, anyway?" asks the author of the introduction to *Literacy
for Life*. Following this is a series of questions such as, "What
are the needs of literacy in our time?" and "What are the salient
characteristics of our students as we assess their potential for
achieving literacy?" (6) These questions, which for all their
Aristotelianism concentrate on the assessment issue, are nota-
ble for several reasons, but their persistence in separating literacy from other issues, as well as separating literates from one
another, is characteristic.

The end of the 1980s has brought few new questions. A
review in *College English* of four recent books concerning literacy asks if literacy is

> to be defined in terms of its potential or its actual practice
> [echoes of Scribner and Cole]. Can the results of becoming
> literate be distinguished from the prerequisites for becom-
> ing literate? Do cultures, subcultures, even individuals differ
> merely in the uses they make of reading and writing, or must
> we more accurately say that they develop different litera-
> cies. . . . (Brandt 129)

The confusion of the thing literacy with the effect of literacy is
apparent. Yet the laying out of questions appears to clarify little
while it delays action.

Two reasons for the tactics seem clear. First, the profession
that asks the questions is itself confused. English educators

have long enjoyed their status partly because of the inexpressibility of what they do. As Delattre indicates, literacy is considered an "inside" phenomenon. Second, the profession has an interest in believing in the enigmatic power of the literate artifact—a sort of homage to the solid demonstration of the result of literacy: the script, the printed page, the preserved manuscript, the student's five-paragraph essay. Literacy possesses and confers powers that reside in and are inseparable from literacy items. John Bormuth, a reading specialist, supplies an unintentional description of this quasi-mysticism. "In what meaningful sense," he asks, "could we say, for example, that a highly skilled reader enjoys literacy when in fact he lives on a desert island and has nothing to read?" (66) To explore this concept of literacy is to demystify a myth.

Another essay from *Literacy for Life*, "The Politics of Literacy," by Sarah Goddard Power, attests ably to the grander aspects of literacy per se. Literacy, according to Power, confers three things:

- As individuals gain reading skills they extend the scope of their experience through print media. Messages in the print media tend to promote change.
- Literacy permits individual receivers, rather than senders, to control the rates at which messages are received, stored, and interpreted.
- Literacy unlocks more complex mental abilities. Whereas the illiterate individual is largely dependent on memory, the literate individual is able to manipulate symbols. (28)

Aside from the fact that all of these assertions are wrong, as Scribner and Cole have shown in spite of their difficulties, they evidence an appeal to literacy that hardly stops short of supplication. This mentality, no doubt, figures into Power's final lament apropos of the incivility of illiteracy. As she says, "the devastating truth about literacy [is that] regardless of the nature of the society, an illiterate cannot function successfully within it" (22).

Power's point is not to be dismissed entirely; she undoubtedly speaks for many of the nonpoor and nonilliterate in the society. No one would argue, either, that illiteracy in a highly technologized society is irrelevant to the situation of the illiterate. On the contrary, the argument is that a highly literate society that withholds literacy from some of its members uses literacy as another form of exploitation. The exploitation, however, does not come about because of magical qualities of literacy to transport, or fail to transport, an individual or community from marginalization to decent conditions of lives and opportunities.

In 1970, in his book *Crisis in the Classroom*, Charles Silberman attributes the overall demise in education to the "mindlessness" of teachers (81). Silberman is not even being critical. Practicing teachers, however, have rarely been consulted about their profession, and late-twentieth-century tactics have tended less to bring in teachers than to spread the responsibility for knowing about teaching to other fields. Today, the crisis in literacy education could be attributed to more and diverse academic professionals and researchers "minding" their lessons. In this respect, another group of academics concerned with literacy has emerged. They have achieved a high profile because they build their case on unorthodox views of what literacy is and on who inherits the right to question long-standing traditions.

Included, in addition to people like Scribner and Cole, are others whose disciplines are psychology, sociology, linguistics, or anthropology. It is telling that this group adopts a fairly controversial form of research. The prevailing form is ethnography. It is ethnographic research on literacy to which we now turn.

Ethnography basically comes from anthropology (at least a branch of anthropology) and involves the firsthand collection and evaluation of data by observers. In this respect, ethnography is ripe for an investigation of ideology. A title in a social-work publication indicates the possibilities. "Blitzkrieg Ethnography" warns of the dangers of placing the observer on a pedestal (Rist; see also Kantor et al.). Indeed, one of the great difficulties of discussing the claims of ethnographic research is the research method itself. We might proceed with care, then, to make clear distinctions between the practice of ethnography and the possibilities it suggests. Some ethnographies are better than others; to understand why requires a general assessment of the motives for ethnographic research.

Aside from Scribner and Cole's use of ethnography, perhaps the most forceful argument for its use comes from the work of Shirley Brice Heath. Heath is a leading Western researcher in the field of language and literacy. Her book *Ways with Words* has undoubtedly changed the ways English researchers look at literacy as well as ways to do research. *Ways with Words* more than anything else traces the stories of language in communities. Her milieu is a small Southern town that she studied for ten years. Three communities within the town attract her attention; she studies poor black communities, mill communities, and mainstream communities. Based on lengthy and persistent observation, Heath is able to show the powerful strategies of community language. She makes the case that certain ways with language are esteemed according to their usefulness within communities, but that the power of the ways with language is dependent upon the power of the communities. Many of these ways, therefore, constitute barriers to full participation in the mainstream (dominant) society for people who do not speak or write the mainstream language.

Heath shows that systematic patterns of language from childhood through adulthood emerge along clear, often chilling, lines. She says in the epilogue to her book:

> Long before reaching school, children of the townspeople [the mainstream community] have made the transition from the home to the larger societal institutions which share the values, skills, and knowledge bases of the school. Their eventual positions of power in the school and the workplace are foredestined in the conceptual structures which they have learned at home and which are reinforced in school and numerous other associations. (368)

These transitions, Heath argues, are paved with language. So, she asks of her nonmainstream constituency:

> Will the road ahead be altered for the students [of black and mill families] who have, through the efforts of some of their teachers, learned to add to their ways of using a language at home? Will their school acquired habits of talking about ways of knowing, reporting on uses of language, and reading and writing for a variety of functions and audiences be transmitted to their children? (362)

Heath's answer is more pessimistic than not. She believes that changes will be long in coming and will require changes in both schools and jobs. She cites particularly the kinds of jobs that render employees "unable to make changes in the procedures for accomplishing a task, and often not privileged to know the outcome of a project . . . " (365). Schools, she says, will have to learn to integrate many ways with language if schooling is to

offer equal education to students. All of these recommendations, Heath believes, are validated by ethnographic observation.

Should nonmainstream students adopt "acquired habits"
of language to transform their usual linguistic styles and to
render their offspring more like townspeople? This is the sort of
question that provides entry into broader evaluations of
Heath's work. Like Scribner and Cole, Heath demonstrates an
integrity that separates her work from the rest, but also like
Scribner and Cole, she succumbs to certain ideological, aca-
demically ratified imperatives that enervate her conclusions.
Scribner and Cole's conclusions are limited by a fixation on
literacy; Heath's by a fixation on language. It is worth a
moment to explore how this happens, since after Heath, as
after Scribner and Cole, it happens again and again.

Heath's argument goes somewhat like this: language is culture; culture is a matter of private, idiosyncratic but embedded
practices and habits; the way to change culture is to change
language; the direction of cultural change should be toward the
mainstream. Within this framework, ideas about society (politics) elide ideas about culture because the relativity of language
is too complicated to be accommodated by schools. Thus, our
duty is to transform plurality into acceptability, to facilitate
conformity. To put it another way, if we teach students to
communicate in mainstream ways, then society will become
more equal and just.

This argument is often tacit in Heath's work; when it sur-
faces it is accompanied by corroborative statements about how
language patterns are formed. On the other hand, Heath appears to find logic in the dominant ways with words. She
acknowledges, for example, that mainstream parents bring up
their children in "contexts that [reflect] the systemic relationships between education and production" (368). (Heath is not
claiming a plot between education and production, of course,
but she certainly suggests a rational connection.) She is not as
generous with nonmainstream families. Her description of the
nonmainstream linguistic habits (inutile within the larger society) suggests a blind entrapment in which nonmainstream
families make unrelenting, *linguistic* choices to prolong dises-
tablishment. A rather lengthy but telling quotation captures
this. Heath predicts the future of nonmainstream students:

> The young couples of [the black and mill communities], as
> they build their families, will move away from some of their

parents' habits and ties to the past. But because the home patterns of language use are inextricably linked to other cultural features, a change in those language uses which so powerfully determine a child's success in school and future vocational orientation will come very slowly, and only in concert with numerous other types of change. The ways with words, transmitted across generations, and covertly embedded and intertwined with other cultural patterns, will not change rapidly. Many of these ways with words will continue to be in accord with and to reinforce other cultural patterns, such as space and time orderings, problem-solving techniques, group loyalties, and preferred patterns of recreation. . . . The deep and wide-reaching complexities of language, time, and space are more resistant to change than are single-factor activities. . . . It is through these ways of living, believing, and valuing that the descendants [of nonmainstream families] will unconsciously pass on their knowledge and skills in the symbolic manipulation of language. (366–367)

Of interest here is not merely Heath's mixing of levels of cultural activities but also her idea of what a cultural activity is. The predominance given the notion of space-and-time orderings presumes some basic characteristic of cultural (if not universal) identity. Such a presumption is hardly on a par with ideas about group loyalty expressed in language habits. Heath's definition of "culture," in other words, stretches the imagination—or, perhaps, reveals a tacit imagination. How do "problem-solving techniques" or "space-and-time orderings" participate in cultural determination, determination that in the last instance results in chronic, underfed disfranchisement for large, identifiable groups of people? Will different time-and-space orderings, rendered by changes in linguistic habits, bring opportunity and justice into apparently disordered lives? Heath is ambivalent. On the one hand, she believes that nonmainstream folks will have to practice mainstream habits repeatedly:

Maintenance of . . . [newly acquired mainstream] habits depends on both sustained motivation for entrance into some vocation in which they are seen as relevant, and exposure . . . to multiple situations in which the habits can be repeatedly practiced. (362)

The implication is that mainstreamers are made, not born. On the other hand, she knows that cultural habits do not die easily; "parents [in nonmainstream communities] will initiate changes in their cultures only when they see it as their responsibility to provide opportunities for their children to practice or extend what the school teaches" (363–364).

So, it is the responsibility of parents to recognize the counterproductiveness of their cultural habits, whatever they may be. It is also their responsibility to encourage the formation of new, school-practiced habits. Herein lies a direct contradiction, however. New school habits of literacy (and other culture-linked conventions) are new only for the outside community. Could we not ask if the attempt to habituate nonmainstream children to alien systems of culture might ensure the maintenance of the existing social order? Can one break into justice by acquiring the habits that have promoted injustice?

It is probably not accurate to lump together the opportunities of poor black and poor white communities. Notwithstanding the economic forecast that looms over both of these groups, particularly in the South, simply being white is a step in the door. As Heath implies and would no doubt agree, the actual linguistic habits of Southern whites and blacks are close; economy, however, takes precedence over habits.

Thus, the results of the study reveal an ideology rather than an alternative. A ten-year observation of chronic disparity and bias produces less a call for change in a self-satisfied, mainstream society than a mandate for a despairing people to change their language ways. What is needed is a recognition of the engine of social changes that might alleviate economic demarcation along the fault line of linguistic habits. Like Scribner and Cole's work, therefore, this study preserves the role of language and encourages speakers to adapt to the status quo. Why, we must ask, do studies of language always result in solutions that are linguistic rather than social or economic?

There is a certain apprehension of finding fault with researchers like Heath and Scribner and Cole because, in spite of difficulties, much of what they do focuses our attention on what is to be done. Heath, in particular, since the publication of *Ways with Words* has written and spoken of a number of literacy programs with which she has been connected that promise change and deliver it. Yet change circumscribed by quotidian goals brings its own problems. A recent observation made by Frank Smith, a long-time defender of the accessibility of literacy, chills because it portends just the opposite of linguistic solutions. Smith, at the end of one literacy conference, finds himself compelled to doubt his commitment to the ideals of reading and writing:

> I can no longer regard the benefit of [literacy's] acquisition as axiomatic. Rather, the proposition that literacy is desirable and worth the effort of learning has to be argued and defended—especially, perhaps, with the children we so egocentrically expect to follow our example (or our precept) of literate skills and interests. (Goelman et al., *Awakening to Literacy* v)

The reason that Smith's assessment is so chilling is that his abandonment of literacy rests on the same assumptions as his staunch defense of literacy. Smith has been a long-time advocate of the contextuality of literacy, albeit that contextuality has been middle class. One of his primary messages has been that teachers make literacy difficult. Yet now, because even context seems to have failed, he is bothered by the egocentrism of literacy. Perhaps he has been trying to avail literate opportunities to the wrong people; perhaps the intrinsic good of literacy does not match the intrinsic good of the people who cannot, or will not, learn to read and write. Perhaps he has been availing to the right people the wrong thing; as he says, some "children who receive [successful] formal instruction in reading and writing do not necessarily become literate . . . (*Awakening* vi).

Self-doubt such as Smith's is rare in the literate professions, and it is helpful to study the newest research that stimulates it. Smith is prompted to reassess his commitments on the basis of ethnographic findings. Long aware that cognitive psychology has prevailed in educational issues, Smith appears ready for a fresh perspective. An article in 1982 in *Research in the Teaching of English* comments on the emergence of the ethnographic method:

> Whether you align yourself with the cynics who view the current popularity of ethnographic studies as one more passing research fad or with the ethnographic evangelists who see field investigations as the panacea for all educational problems, you certainly cannot ignore its growing impact on research in English Education. (Kantor, et al. 293)

The authors applaud the new direction:

> This issue of *Research in the Teaching of English* acknowledges the emerging importance of ethnographic studies in English education and examines the methodology, suggesting reasons why it may be the design of choice for many language, composition, literature, and reading studies, particu-

larly those which question basic assumptions about the growth of writing and reading abilities in the classroom. (293)

The freshness of the ethnographic perspective unfortunately may excuse its incompleteness and sidestep an important issue: how ethnographic research presumes to contribute to an understanding of literacy. What, we may ask bluntly, do ethnographers of literacy want? The answer is neither clear nor original. The newest research appears to reinforce the directions of Scribner and Cole and Heath, and to sanction them. New ethnographies recast old ideologies: ethnographic studies confirm, once again, that the subject of their study—literacy—is the barrier as well as the invitation to mainstream life.

A representative example of this confirmation is found in the leadoff article in the 1984 *Awakening to Literacy* (Goelman et al. eds.), a collection of essays that includes Heath and a number of others in the forefront of ethnographic studies. This volume exemplifies certain ethnographic designs and both recommends and proceeds on their bases. It sets the tenor for ethnographic research that is echoed not only within the essay collection but into the future as well.

One essay in the collection is titled, "Learning to Read Culturally: Literacy Before Schooling." The authors, Bambi B. Schieffelin and Marilyn Cochran-Smith, intend the essay to fill a void in the literature (presumably not all literature), to explore "literacy as a social and cultural phenomenon . . . that exists between people and . . . that connects individuals to a range of experiences and to different points of time" (4). The connections that interest Schieffelin and Cochran-Smith are those that occur outside of "formal instruction." Formal instruction basically means school, though school in the essay is a hazy idea.

The design of Schieffelin and Cochran-Smith's study is startling. In its broadest outline, it conjoins three educational groups: American preschoolers, a New Guinean mother and her young daughter (preschool in a largely nonschooled society), and a Vietnamese refugee family whose son attends the second grade. The preschool kindergartners come from Philadelphian families whose children, ages 3 to 5, attend nursery school in the area in which they live. The New Guinea family belongs to the Kaluli tribe in the Papuan province, and the Vietnamese family resides in West Philadelphia. The connection among these groups is difficult to ascertain. Ostensibly, preliteracy, or lack of formal training in literacy, stabilizes their relationships. The kindergartners have never been taught to read programmatically; the Papuan mother has attended missionary school but "teaches" literacy to her child during daily, informal routines; and the Vietnamese family consists of "preliterate" adults, i.e., second-language adults who are not literate in English, and a preliterate child who learns English literacy at school but who "informally" teaches English at home.

but also, presumably, not in Vietnamese either.

The "before-schooling" link among these groups appears tenuous at best. A more logical assumption is that the connections are provided by the ethnographers themselves. It is the ethnographers who live or who spent time in Philadelphia and the Papuan province, and it is they who have superimposed the idea of preschool on these various groups. Ideas of preschool, preliterate, and formal programs are thus conveniences as much as realities. They are pressed into service without regard to the differences between literacy education not merely among countries but within political exigencies. We never know whether or not the Vietnamese family went to school in Vietnam.

An equally puzzling facet of the study's design is the reference to the social class of the members of the communities. Class appears to play a large role for the ethnographers. They make much of their own middle class status as they prepare to avoid middle class biases, yet they give no indication about what those biases might be. In fact, the profession of middle class status amounts to an extrication from its confines. (We might recall the disintegration of class taxonomy in the Lynd and Warner studies.) Class, for the ethnographers, appears to be any feature popular in the repertoire of American denial of class. For example, the kindergartners are said to represent the middle class; this means that the parents have "strikingly similar educational backgrounds" and many of the mothers teach school (5). At the same time, these kindergartner families possess diverse heritages; the families are "white Eastern and Western European, Jewish, Indian, Filipino, Egyptian, English, and Black American" (5). In addition, some of the children in the middle class are bilingual or monolingual in a non-English language. Even within the collective ken of token American classism, these features stretch many boundaries. The in-country class status of the non-American families, the Papuans or the Vietnamese, is never mentioned.

check this claim + what it means?

The mention of class becomes understandable only when one realizes that class is already assumed to be a function of literacy. Indeed, what really defines the class of these divergent groups is their literate experience. The members of the middle class "expect" their children to become literate, whereas this expectation is more abstruse in other contexts. Surely, in this respect, the ethnographers are on to something, but the something is exactly what the ethnographers must set out to discover, not take for granted. As the ethnographers haggle over the irrelevancies of class identification, their own biases emerge.

For example, within the general design of the study, an odd but ubiquitous feature is an inconsistent relationship between the observers and those observed. No member of the American middle class group, for example, is referred to by surname; the references are always plural. The Kaluli family, however, is referred to specifically by name, first name, in fact. The Vietnamese child (and family) is referred to by initials, as is his teacher, Miss K. The child, furthermore, is said to live in the lower class section of town, where he goes to school with other refugees like himself—"Indian, Haitian, Ethiopian" (16). Refugees of different ethnicities possess unique histories, however, as well as different refugee statuses and experiences. Refugees cannot simply be massed together unless all the observers see is a mass. The labeling may seem a piddling matter, but, in fact, is part and parcel of the larger failure to identify the bases of class or the empirical ground rules on which class research goes forward.

Characterizations of each study are also peculiar. The different studies are validated according to the length of time they are studied. The kindergartners were studied for 18 months. The Kaluli were observed as part of a larger study, but the literacy information comes from "83 hours of transcribed and annotated conversations" and "extensive interviews and observations" (23). The Vietnamese work is not put in a time frame, although it is apparent that the child is observed at school and is accompanied home by the ethnographer on several occasions. Undoubtedly, accounting for time, transcription, and paper collection is a habit of ethnographic process. On the other hand, within the assumption of ethnography that knowledge is contextual and understood as a matter of value rather than account, the enumeration of hours and calendars is discomforting. Furthermore, when the ethnographers set out to view literacy in "relevant contexts," these contexts *become* the hours; the depth of context rarely gets a hearing.

This is the sort of problem that underlies the design difficulties. Ethnocentrism, here as in other studies, effaces ethnographic questions about the content of a literacy event. Literacy, indeed, is defined prior to context and transported from scene to scene like a suitcase; once in place, the notetaking begins. "Literacy events" are events in which literacy occurs. So, one asks, what is literacy? In this study, literacy is described as a "cultural phenomenon that interacts with certain sociological processes" (4). What is the phenomenon? The phenomenon, unsurprisingly, is print. Literacy is a litany of print: "books and literacy-related activities" (3), "texts and other printed materials" (6), "books and book-related items" (6), "name labels . . . books and other printed materials . . . printed stories . . . the fictional narratives of storybooks and . . . [the] print of posters, signs, and labels" (7), "simple booklets with line drawings" (11), "each black and white page" (13), "books and magazines" (19), "print" (21). These events generalize to New Guinea as well as to the Philadelphia refugee household and include transcribed speech. Literacy is the object in the environment that connects all environments; it is coterminous in all aspects of display and resource. It may be published by American corporate textbook makers of children's stories; produced by students of ages three or nine, Egyptian or Vietnamese; written and distributed by missionaries; found on walls or within bindings. Literacy is universal; in this study, content is also.

Practice or use, of course, is the auspice that explains the appearance of the artifact, the event that demands the literacy. What happens in ethnography, however, is that practice never gets a hearing, either. Practice is a formality. The ethnographers observe in the kindergarten, for example, literacy events without content:

> There was no incongruity between a nursery school philosophy that deemphasized early reading and writing and a pervasion of printed materials and print-related activities in the nursery school setting itself. There was no incongruity because the context of nursery school literacy events almost never was instruction or situations wherein adults attempted to teach children to read or write. Rather, literacy events consistently were embedded within the routine interactions of adults and children. For participants, the literacy events themselves were not noteworthy. (7)

The event, in other words, acquires its own autonomy, separate from content and historical context.

On this issue, Scribner and Cole claimed ignorance of historical theory to account for practices they could not understand. Schieffelin and Cochran-Smith, however, claim everything as an explanation. The relativity of practice and the parity of literacy events mean that literacy can have any use. They give numerous examples. The middle class uses run the relative gamut:

> Families used printing and found print to be appropriate in a large number of contexts. In this community, unlike other social groups, there was no single context in which literacy could occur and no single purpose to which it could be put. (6)

Such are the virtues of a universal literacy, to serve meaning in all "contexts and for many purposes in . . . everyday lives" (8). Even small children use literacy according to their "own social purposes . . . to effectively fulfill their own needs" (9). This is not to propose indifference to childhood needs; yet lost within the generality of needs are their history, gravity, development, and so on. Lost is the overdetermination of needs; the Vietnamese child, for example, represses his needs by keeping them secret (17). Children, adults, and all in between have needs or uses for literacy. Some needs are not just any needs, however.

The problem gains significance when we take into account the model of society operant in Western ethnography. The most succinct way to put it is the ethnographers' own; they are interested to discover the meaning of "what literacy means to the individuals involved" (4). Society, to these ethnographers, is individuality multiplied; it is composed of autonomous persons who determine their needs for literacy independently. When individuals aggregate, culture adds up; therefore, individual needs are cultural needs. What Schieffelin and Cochran-Smith appear not to grasp is that societies precede individuals. Indeed, even ethnographers come from a culture, or a society, that traps them when they do not ask what the society obtains for them—no matter the wish to be autonomous. This is ideology. Schieffelin and Cochran-Smith simply aver to rote explanations of larger ideas of culture: "We suggest that a careful examination of cross-cultural material may allow us to reevaluate the way we have formulated prerequisites for the achievement of literacy which have been based on the experiences of a relatively small number of social groups" (4). But what groups and why them? The narrowness of the prevailing concept of literacy appears to these ethnographers as unfortunate happenstance. They would seem to believe that more knowledge of more literacies will yield greater social (and economic?) tolerance. Why this should be so, or how knowledge of uses of literacy would change the methods of American education and/or global commerce, is unclear. Indeed, in this ethnography, the needs of literacy disengaged from the most ingrained (thus the most tacit) Western uses—to please and to educate—appear unfathomable or pathetic. Three examples in the Schieffelin/Cochran-Smith ethnography show this to be true.

The middle class needs appear without incident. Middle class people expect certain effects of literacy to occur naturally. Middle class parents teach their children to read storybooks as leisurely entertainment and to problem-solve, to introduce and verify "new" information, and, as one middle class mother says, to validate knowledge of "just about everything" (6). Literacy provides an outlet for childhood emotions; literacy allows middle class children to "sort out and work through strong feelings" (7).

The Kaluli family in New Guinea, however, appears to use literacy for nothing. The inclusion of the Kaluli in the essay itself requires a sympathetic ear; the Kaluli's literacy before schooling appears to be literacy after missionaries, which, in the usual sense, does not coincide. The outlines of the Kaluli study are broader than literacy, of course. Over a number of years, this preliterate society has been observed, ostensibly for its orality since the ethnographers characterize the society "as an egalitarian one in which face-to-face interactions predominate" (11). The current ethnographers, however, take particular interest in a preliterate family, one of whose members is a preliterate daughter who appears to solicit literate interaction with the mother. The daughter is two years old. The upshot of the literacy events between mother and daughter amounts to very little, in any event. The ethnographers observe that "literacy activities for the Kaluli are very suggestive, but they have little connection to other aspects of social life. Looking at books is seen as neither instructional nor entertaining" (14). The mother and daughter share a missionary Bible pamphlet, for example, but the mother does not encourage "her child to look at the book and she did not use any of the attentionals (such as 'look!')" which, for the ethnographers, constitute an act of reading (being literate) (13). Thus, the ethnographers agree with the mother, who says that "literacy is to no purpose" (15). The mother, of course, is probably right, but probably because she has a different idea of purpose than those who observe her. She also may have a different view of two-year-old children.

Indeed, there are Western purposes that literacy propagates, and their impact is clear. According to the ethnographers,

> those villagers who were interested and participated [in the literacy instruction at the mission/government school] separated themselves from those who continued to lead more traditional lives. . . . [Moreover], anyone attending the mission would have difficulty gardening and performing other food-collecting activities, and so other family members who did not participate in literacy activities would have to provide food for those who did become involved in literacy and mission activities. This could present a problem in a society where people are organized to supply food for members of their households. (12)

Further, as if more evidence is needed of literacy's impact, the ethnographers add, "Interest in literacy tended to separate individuals from one another in fairly significant ways and changed the usual patterns of organizing social activities" (12). Yet literacy is to no purpose.

The Vietnamese refugee setting provides the third demonstration of the Western view to literacy; in some ways, its view is the most internalized. In this situation, the ethnographers come up explicitly against their own ethnocentrism, and disregard it. Aside from the rather contrived circumstance of presuming the preliteracy of the non-English-speaking parents, the discussion centers mostly on the acquisition of literacy by the child. (One of the difficulties of this section is determining whose preliteracy is at issue as well as who teaches whom in formal-vs-informal locations.) Outside of the formal school of the child, none of the usual definitions or explanations of literacy hold. The literacy "eventness" of the home life is veritably nil:

> The family owns a television, and on the weekend often go to Chinatown to see Chinese movies. . . . [T]here are no books on the night tables or magazines on a rack . . . [and] there is no television guide. (17)

At the same time, however, the child is progressing well in literacy at school and he seems not to notice the literacy deprivation of his home life. The ethnographers conclude, therefore, that

> Even if [the family's] environment does not have a variety of books and reading material for them to explore and is not literate in some sense, their ideology is. (21)

The admission is shattering. And completely ignored. In its place stands the absence of a *TV Guide.* Why, we have to ask, would literates be presumed to have a *TV Guide*?

On the basis of the three cases, the study concludes only what it can. It has stripped literacy of content, content of judgment, judgment of social and economic consequence. To wit, literacy attains transparence:

> The variation among the three groups we have examined demonstrates that the concept of literacy has many different meanings and has many implications. Children and adults learn a number of different kinds of literacy in different ways and for different purposes. (21)

Literacy is different, and so is the world, except, of course, as this ethnography indicates, the same is true if literacy is all the same.

Perhaps the above sorts of research efforts would not be as depressing if they did not eclipse the details of social life that are otherwise painful and clear. There is one occasion in the Schieffelin and Cochran-Smith study, for example, when an extended piece of literacy is explored. The Vietnamese child writes a story that the ethnographers reproduce in his hand. Yet the ethnographers focus on the Western conventions of the story to the exclusion of its message. They comment on the significance of its "narrative mode"; they note that the story's theme of literacy competence "is unrepeated by the English speakers in the classroom" (19). But the story consists of more than an ethnographer's "theme" or a composition modality. The story is about a wise man who gives a child (the writer) a magic book whose words the child cannot read; when the child makes known his desire to read, the magic book magically fulfills his wish, and he reads (19). Other occasions of the ethnographers' inattention to the refugee relationship to literacy are also palpable. Whereas the ethnographers conclude that the Vietnamese adults show no sign of ever developing an "involvement in English literature for personal expression or enjoyment," (21) they also note that the occasions for English literacy are bureaucratic—the family must fill out forms, from job applications to tax and hospital forms. The child's contact with literacy at school is such to cause him deep embarrassment when the father misspells a word in a note to the teacher; one of the child's classroom penchants is to point out misspelled words to his classmates. Often, the child accompanies the mother to complete errands or supply translations for the "people whose homes she was cleaning" (17).

Kaluli observations possess similar implications but are less elaborated. The Kaluli's literacy is not even their own script (as it was with the Vai); literacy was first introduced to the Kaluli tribe by "evangelical missionaries" who syllabified the Kaluli language and made it "hard to say" (12–14). The Kaluli children do not learn much literacy in school in any case. This is hardly surprising.

Because there is no place in a Western literacy scheme to castigate the forms of Western literacy, the details of lives dominated—or supported—by the West exist only as background information. They are absorbed into the dominant ideology at just the moment they exhibit or defy the domination—at the literacy event. Thus, the overwhelming importance of the nature, cause, and history of the event is lost, and thus the irony of the authors' final remarks:

> What we wish to impress on the reader is the importance of an ethnographic approach to studying the complex relationships involved in the acquisition and evolution of literacy. Without serious consideration of what literacy means and does not mean for those people who are introduced to it, it will be impossible to make sense of the ways literacy organizes and is organized by different social groups. (22)

The ethnographic method, as evidenced by this study, announces the inability to make sense out of literacy.

This assessment may be overstated, but not by much. It is more than merely unkind to reduce non-Westerners to aimless moviegoers or tribes to undistinguished comprehenders. None of these studies—Scribner and Cole, Heath, Schieffelin and Cochran-Smith—sets out to do so; yet each study delivers the practice of literacy into a universal realm of infinite interpretation. Scribner and Cole point to the sociohistorical system for an understanding of the consequences of literacy. Heath scales the meaning down to a community level, the political value of literacy to the mainstream population. And Schieffelin and Cochran-Smith locate the meaning within the individual even as the individual exists within a community within a class, within a society, within a culture. Yet, whereas none of these locations is wrong and all are material, the impetus for each study has been to separate out literacy from its environs for its presumed uniqueness. Thus, literacy has attained a stature unto itself; it exists spatially, technically, and neutrally, or it does not exist at all. This is to say that the literacy flag signals itself first.

This confusion between the apparent concreteness of the object and the groundlessness of its symbolicity results in the helplessness of these ethnographic conclusions. For the ethnographers, their task is done when literacy is excised; when society gets in the way, they say so and delegate the more difficult questions to other disciplines (though in the meantime they simplify society). That the ethnographic data often contains in it the answers to the socioeconomic nature of literacy but that these are not seen is a function of the ideology that oppresses both the researchers and their subjects.

Some aspects of the ethnographic approach and its underlying assumptions have been called into question. In *Theory and Resistance in Education: A Pedagogy for the Opposition*, Henry Giroux writes of the strange enervation of literacy in the current American educational debate:

> Literacy is an issue that in the current debate regarding the role and purpose of schooling appears to have "escaped" from the ideologies that inform it. At first glance, there is a curious paradox in the fact that while the subject of literacy has once again become a major educational issue, the discourse that dominates the debate represents a conservative retreat from dealing with the issue in a significant way—the scope and widespread interest in literacy and schooling has generally served to flatten the debate rather than enhance it. With few exceptions, the issue of literacy has been removed from the broader social, historical, and ideological forces that constitute its existence. (205)

Giroux's assessment of the situation proves particularly useful as an antidote to in-house provincialism; more than this, Giroux is concerned to reinvest literacy with a political content and status. As he says,

> the ideology that informs conventional conceptions of literacy has stripped it of its function for critical reasons, as a

mode of thought and assemblage of skills that allow individuals to break with the predefined.... [Literacy] has been
reduced to the alienating rationality of the assembly line, a
mastery without benefit of comprehension or political insight. (206)

Giroux is also aware that "literacy can be neither neutral nor
objective, and that for the most part ... is inscribed in the
ideology and practice of domination" (225).

Giroux's observations are in the main correct and distinguish him from the many scholars who subscribe to a definition of literacy in the usual manner. But, implicit within
Giroux's critique lies the usual definition itself. When he
speaks of "stripping" literacy, itself an "assemblage of skills"
whose self-possessed political status is "inscribed in" ideology,
he adheres to the vision of a reified literacy. The difference with
Giroux is that literacy is abstracted to a higher level; instead of
graffiti and captions on poster paper, Giroux speaks of reading
and writing comprehension. Print does not dominate; comprehension of print does. To comprehend, in Giroux's model, is to
perceive ideas within words (symbols). This is a difficult idea
to disentangle, and the problem leads Giroux to the second
abyss of previous researchers and that is the separation of literacy from the social matrix that gives it meaning. He splits the
ideology of literacy into two camps. These are the instrumental
and interactionist views of literacy. Their characters, respec-
tively, carry the dual Western mandates of literacy—to educate
and to please.

The instrumental approach to understanding and impart-
ing literacy takes a positivist, conservative position. It deals
with literacy as a method to instill knowledge. Giroux summarizes, "The major premises of instrumental ideology are drawn
from the logic and method ... of prediction, efficiency, and
technical control derived from eighteenth-century science"
(210). The knowledge to be dispensed is the best knowledge, of
course—good books—and the writing to be demonstrated is
formal. Good students possess exemplary abilities to exem-
plify. The instrumental approach is top down and factorylike.
In contrast, the interactionist approach assumes a romantic
stance. It is placid and individualistic. It leans on a cognitive,
developmental model in which power is reduced to a struggle
or interaction between "man and the natural world.... In the
romantic [emotional] approach, power is reduced to the discourse of psychological categories and ends up becoming

synonymous with concepts such as 'self-fulfillment,' 'becoming,' and 'self-actualization' " (219).

In both instrumental and interactionist approaches, literacy is held to possess intrinsic rather than allusive properties. Giroux says,

> The result is a view of literacy that celebrates an abstract condition regarding language use ... [and] removes the notions of roles, rationality, and culture, all of which deeply structure the school experience, from the benefit of sociological and historical analysis. (221)

The effects of both of the ideologies are the same. The interactionist approach works to "divorce theory from practice and consciousness from social action ... reduc[ing] the relationships between content and context either to the imperatives of feeling good or to the safety of the classroom debate" (220). At the same time, the instrumental approach defines knowledge as "objective, outside of the existence of the knower, and subject to the demands of exact and precise formulation" (210).

Giroux turns from literacy per se to the domination of the schools. In school, he assumes that comprehension equals the intake of information and ideology. This is how schools turn out proper conformity and regulate failure. As a piece of weaponry in the ideological arsenal, literacy enforces acceptable ideas and behaviors: "In essence, language practices represent one feature of the dominant culture that schools legitimate in varying degrees" (214). To a certain extent, Giroux is right. He is at least right to pursue the location of meaning across the domain of schooling. He is also right to point out that students come to school with the "values, styles, taste, and culture of the favored classes" already favored (214). Mainstream literate students are rewarded for their submission to certain literate habits. But students do not submit to language. Literacy is not a blunt instrument of domination. It is, as Giroux says, "a political phenomenon ... [that] represents an embattled epistemological terrain on which different sociological groups struggle over how reality is to be signified, reproduced, and resisted" (237).

Fighting over sociological signification is a linguistic fight inseparable from the politics of schooling, however. Literacy, as Giroux mistakenly assumes, is not a mirror of educational battles; it is the battle. One suspects that Giroux views the indoctrination of literacy as something that happens only during an English class. No doubt literacy's oppression may be realized there, but it is not limited to spelling, grammar, and vocabulary tests. The fact is that citizenship courses (a special interest of Giroux), history, science, and other subjects also demarcate students according to literate achievement. Students who do not learn to read or write do not learn history, science, or the intricacies of literate citizenship. The question boils down to how the preservation of canonical literacy for one group of students works to its benefit while the vocationalization of literacy for a group of other students works to its detriment.

It may be asked of the present analysis if it is not guilty itself of, at least, rarefying and abstracting literacy. Have we not effaced literacy, questioned its presence and purpose, and attacked or discarded it? The answer is that until the basis for our current approach to and understanding of literacy is examined, our questions will generate the kinds of nonanswers that we have seen and they will continue to block further understanding and action. They will lead to the study of literacy, on the one hand, in the most microscopic of ways, and, on the other, to the study of purpose and practice in the most uninformed, ideologically covert manner. These are precisely the directions of most current literacy discussion. One final example should serve to illustrate.

In "The Ethnography of Literacy," an essay in *Writing: The Nature, Development, and Teaching of Written Communication* (Whiteman, ed.), John F. Szwed latches on to the dualities of literacy in the most ferocious way. Apropos of the objective artifactuality of literacy, Szwed expresses concern that we may not be paying enough attention to print. He is concerned that we do not take seriously matters of *typography:* One small but important example is the current debate over the widespread use of Helvetic type (as used by Amtrak, Arco, Mobil, and numerous other business and governmental sign and logo users). The issue turns on whether the commercial type—presumably depersonalized, authoritative, and straightforward—brings unfair and misleading pressure to bear on its readers, since it appears to be the face of the largest and most powerful forces in America (17). Indeed, Szwed suspects, if typeface could swing a stick, consumers had better duck.

Turning from the specific to the ideologically general, Szwed ponders why and how reading and writing are done. His statements reveal some sweeping assumptions:

> A quick beginning inventory of reading contexts would include bedside reading, coffee-break and lunch-time reading, vacation reading, reading to children, Sunday reading (perhaps the day of most intense literary activity in the United States and Europe), reading during illness, educational reading (both in institutions and informally), crisis reading (psychological, physical, spiritual), sexual reading, reading to memorize, commuter reading, reading to prevent interaction with others, etc. In theory, at least, there is a form of reading specific to every room: books are sold for kitchens, coffee tables, desks, bedrooms ... or bathrooms. (17–18)

Szwed's idea of context and purpose is rather complete, one might say, given that one lives in a nice Western house with a nine-to-five job, psychological self-doubts, and well-lit bathrooms. This is a world that exists, no doubt, but it is a world of Western platitudes as well as a demonstration of American academic arrogance. Not everyone lives in Szwed's house, and the most pressing issues of literacy do not reside there either.

Within the confines of a critique on literacy research, one must assert that the current modes will not do. To define literacy and then proceed to look for it is not merely to lose the possibility of discovery but to forget that those possibilities exist. It is also to forget that research itself exists within a set of academic, economic, and political relationships. Researchers are part of the world they want to examine; at the same time, they set themselves outside of and in superior relationship to selected bits of the world, be they Vai society, ghetto Philadelphia, or American schools. The researcher is the adjudicator, the one who turns the other into an object. The researcher must ask, therefore, why she or he is in a position to do so and what may be the consequences of his or her actions.

In large measure, these are not questions that have been asked in the research under review here. They are, of course, the questions that must be asked. Their range is broad, tortuous, and dangerous. To begin where we are is to ask first about the usefulness of recent research on literacy that ends without ways to explain use as a fully operative, integrated concept. Scribner and Cole, for example, find not one but three literacies in a society, each with a specified "use," but, more important, each with a significance for the other. Yet most of their research time was spent on distinguishing one literacy from the other through discrete activity rather than on trying to understand the mesh of activities.

Harder questions than this arise. The first is why study literacy at all? Why, indeed, at this time has literacy become a central issue, a "literacy crisis" its central feature?

Some responses, of course, prefer to dodge the issue by explaining that Americans can read and write as well or as badly as they ever could. But this answer hardly relieves the need to ask or explains the claims for a "crisis." Returning to the original observations about the social base in chapter one, we might keep before us the fact that the relationships among Americans are established along economic lines. Would it not be logical then that literacy conforms also to these lines? Illiterates work for literates in the United States; in undeveloped illiterate countries the same is true. Is it the case that literacy is an economy?

The answer is that literacy is not quite that; money and words are not the same. The chief argument of the present analysis, however, is that literacy and economy are interdependent and that the basis of the economy is changing. Such is the case with literacy—it is an unstable idea, despite our efforts to stabilize it. The nature of the change concerns the shift from industry to information. Given the purposes of the proprietors of the shift, the position in which businesses, corporations, and governmental agencies find themselves is very difficult. Words are neither machines nor products in any usual sense. Yet the reaction to this shift certainly finds part of its expression within the old industrial model. And, since many of the information-based demands of the current technology are more autonomic than creative, the adaptation works.

Literacy can be instrumentalized to a degree, just as people can be. The growing problem is along the boundaries, for there the conceptual difficulties arise: information relates; it does not command. The old world of literacy is in transition. The Western ideology of American academics (and the British, most visibly) no longer suffices; old-guard literates will have to discover new ways to ratify their privileges, and many will lose them. At the same time, as current trends in labor attest, other groups used to privileges will also have to change; they will be forced, at the least, to realign and to retrain. Such is what amounts to the breakdown between white- and blue-collar distinctions. Literacy thus comes to assume a credential status; on it will depend the morbidity of entire groups of workers. As this occurs, the credential itself will lose value as well as content. High school diplomas will mean little; college diplomas will mean little; both will be required. The point is, however, that the credential, particularly the literacy presumed by the credential, is not the cause of opportunity. Opportunity is merely changing its face.

Are we to presume, then, that literacy education and research can be understood to operate as an instrument of a dominant, funded part of our society? Is there an evil overlay to our current research activities? As vulgar as the question may be, it cannot be dismissed. The question is vulgar because literacy is conceived vulgarly—as something that contains its own rights and whose rights can be co-opted. There is nothing overly complicated, in other words, between the needs of a capital economy and the purposes and practices in literacy education. Two examples of their compatibility, if not the outright demand for matching goals, suffice.

The first comes from Richard Lanham, who writes of the purposes of a college composition curriculum. In the 1984 edition of the Modern Language Association publication *Profession*, Lanham calls on composition programs, essentially, to wake up to their agendas:

> Our present bemusement with technology has blinded us to the more fundamental adjustment universities must now make, a response to our information society parallel to the nineteenth-century response to industrialism. I have not been able to invent a stirring phrase for what is needed, and the one I press into service—humanistic engineering—is bound to vex everybody. The thing needed, however, stands clear enough, even if we haven't yet a proper name for it—a curriculum that will focus on our society's demand for ever greater and more complex kinds of verbal symbolization. I have no objection to calling this area simply "rhetoric," if that is not too dirty a word for you. That a service-oriented information society will need a substantial and fundamental education in rhetoric seems beyond question. This broad and unstoppable historical requirement creates the large force, the plate tectonic, of which the literacy crisis, the back-to-basics movements in the schools, and the confusion and disarray of the humanistic curriculum are the most visible symptoms. (12)

"Unstoppable historical" forces are tough competitors, like hurricanes, perhaps. Only when we ask how societies, in fact, stop or begin do we enter a realm in which rhetoric is not only not dirty but plain.

There is an opposite end to Lanham's argument that is equally disturbing, however. Instead of gearing up to meet economic mandates, some foresee gearing down. In the jaws of an information age, perhaps teachers should learn retreat and teach it to their students. This kind of defeatism echoes in an essay by Eleanor Duckworth, who participated in a Harvard symposium concerning the demise of education. She says,

> Given the employment prospects, one might even accept the responsibility to educate young people to live productively while unemployed. This I put forward not altogether in jest. [There are] a number of nonacademic abilities quite as demanding as the arts and sciences: how to identify worthwhile and possible tasks; how to participate in public decision making; how to benefit from local facilities and amenities; how to negotiate with resource holders. None of these is a simple accomplishment. . . . All would be valuable for employed people as well as unemployed. All would contribute to a workable society. (17)

All would contribute to maintaining the need to train students for unemployment, too, if undertaken in the present economic environment. To be sure, Duckworth recalls the vicious realities that not only affect numbers of people in this society but that always have. The separation of educational matters—arts and sciences—from matters of society, however, is the reason, not the cure, for the debilitation of many of society's citizens.

Of course, there are those like Christopher Jencks, who, after completing a massive study, *On Inequality in American Schools*, concludes that nothing the schools do can change children's prospects, and that the only successful "campaign for reducing inequality probably requires that the exploited must cease to accept their condition as inevitable and just" while the rich, for their part, "must begin to feel ashamed of economic inequality" (265). In the event that Jencks's proposals do not work out, literacy educators and researchers have a choice to make. Literacy is part and parcel a relationship that involves the vertical and horizontal exchanges of the means of livelihood in a literate society. Thus, it is the relationships of literacy, which a society bent on unequal distribution of wealth and power dominates completely, that literacy educators must understand in order to proceed in ways that do not implicate them in the domination. Likewise, they should recognize the pitfall of "neutrality" and "objectivity," which may lead to bad faith.

On April 12, 1985, in an interview on National Public Radio, William Labov made two broad statements. First, he said that his most recent research showed a further distancing of ghettoized black language from white, standard English. Second, he said that sociolinguists such as he could not make judgments about the social response to his findings. Labov said that he sees his job as one in which he must lay out the facts. That is true; it is one of his jobs. But he, as well as other literacy scholars, undertakes a second job every time he chooses to go into a ghetto to tape-record and analyze the speech of black people in the United States. This is a political choice, not merely another choice. He cannot claim impunity for consequences he allows by supposing that his is the right to neutrality in a racist society.

The neutral stance of literacy educators and researchers is the ideology that literacy research perpetuates, the mask that allows masking to go on. Neutrality is a claim about form, and the very simplest fact about literacy is that it is always contextual. It is always about something, a content, a subject. Content is the least acknowledged, least talked about, least valued aspect of most of the current research on literacy. Content has been reduced to form and form to relativity, and this has allowed discourse about literacy to proceed without regard to what people are saying. It substitutes concern for material consequences with concern for proprietary boundaries.

In this country, the shift from industry to information takes precedence over the life of the person who "handles" it. Within the Western tradition, as we have seen, there is a belief that something about literacy vehemently opposes the view of life as a commodity. This belief has been useful in ensuring the pleasantness of some lives, and it is not necessarily a wrong belief; at the same time, it has pushed many into the margins. We may want to believe that something about literacy resists domination; what we have to believe is that literacy is an idea our society has not yet finished with. A broader view of literacy that sees it as contextualized, and sees context as economic at heart, may constitute the possibility for change as well as a means. The question is how long the possibility can survive.

Anthony Wilden, Lewis Thomas, Gregory Bateson, Michel Foucault, Theodor Adorno, Karl Kraus, Kenneth Burke, and others distinguish humankind from other kinds of life by the ability of humans to make language. In *System and Structure,* Wilden summarizes:

What probably distinguishes human communication, of which language is an integral part, from all other levels of communications ... especially in the sense that it is far removed or displaced from self-evident or strictly biological survival value—is that the primary goal of human communication appears to be the invention of goals. (431)

This description is optimistic, idealistic, and ridden with the fixation on the autonomy of language just denounced. Language invents nothing on its own. Yet Wilden and others recognize that many goals in this society involve repression which masks as opportunity. The anti-ideological task of those concerned with literacy is to understand how literacy figures into repression and how literacy can change goals. This is to say that we must understand our world in order to do something about our literacy, two tasks that proceed simultaneously.

CHAPTER THREE

THEORIES OF LITERACY AND SOCIETY

◆

As this study has tried to show, the current understanding of literacy is ideological precisely when it fails to disengage itself from the exploitation of illiterates and the loss of opportunities for wider access to knowledge and self- and social consciousness, if not control. These consequences, as Anthony Wilden would say, are a form of social violence. Social violence is, he says,

> a covert form which is perhaps most devastating of all for those subject to it. [It] is the passive violence of the refusal to recognize overt or real violence. It may be expressed in deeds; or in positions, stances, attitudes, rules, codes, manners, in inertia, cynicism, "scientific objectivity," coyness, humor; in refusal, disavowal, negation, or disconfirmation—but also and especially at all levels, in words. (481)

Wilden does not narrow the field of words to literacy, but the power of words is the power of literacy. Literacy is not newly oppressive, but the forms of its violence are.

Literacy is a social restriction and an individual accomplishment. Individuals read and write, or don't, and individuals do with their literacy what they can. The subjectivities of minds and the ways in which people make their lives and thoughts, and the ways in which people are coerced, entrapped, colonized, or freed, must be addressed as processes. At the same time, the processes must not become the issue, since the conditions for any process, and especially for the literacy process, determine the possible outcomes. That is why, for example, teaching literacy depends on the circumstances rather than on the textbook. Our attention needs to be focused on the conditions in every instance.

A theory of literacy is, thus, a theory of society, of social relationships; and the validity of a theory of literacy derives from the actual lives of the people who make the society. It is not the case that literacy provides the key to understanding the connections of a people; it is the case that literacy provides a view from which to survey the history and future of social formations. The theory in this study is that literacy is a system of oppression that works against entire societies as well as against certain groups within given populations and against individual people. The third world is oppressed by the system of literacy of the first world; ghetto blacks are oppressed by the American system of literacy education; and a second-grade girl is oppressed by a teacher who fails to understand the craziness of the spelling of vocabulary words. Literacy oppresses, and it is less important whether or not the oppression is systematic and intentional, though often it is both, than that it works against freedom. Thus, the questions of literacy are questions of oppression; they are matters of enforcement, maintenance, acquiescence, internalization, revolution. Which is to say that when societies dissolve the forms of oppression against their own citizens and against other societies, then they will dissolve the questions of literacy also. Only when the forms of oppression are undermined can the question of what to do with one's life become central.

The engagement between society and individual is what must be understood if literacy is to contribute toward goals of betterment. Chaim Perelman in *The New Rhetoric*, for example, speaks of a "community of minds" that agrees to certain rules of argument and thus functions on the basis of those agreements (55). Communities of minds is an appealing notion; yet negotiations among minds amount to struggles between those who can win and those who cannot. To put it another way, in American society the struggle is between those who can read and write and those who cannot or have no opportunity to, and the struggle is over who is entitled to negotiate. It is perfectly evident which minds do not possess that right. As we explore theories of literacy in society, the ideas of individuality and social relationships themselves come into question.

The work of Paulo Freire, whose own task has been to analyze these questions, provides a useful baseline for discussion. Freire is a revolutionary, but within the world of Brazilian and Chilean peasants, he opts for knowledge over death, literacy over guns. The reappropriation by the illiterate peasant of his own power will occur in direct recognition of, then confrontation with, those who would take his life away. But Freire says this will occur "by means of culture. Cultural action and cultural revolution, at different stages, constitute the modes of this expulsion" of domination (*Politics of Education* 53). For Freire, becoming literate, in a literate society, is the first step to knowing culture.

Although Freire has his limitations, and even his friends speak of the "Brazilian" character of Freire's academic discourse (Giroux xviii), his arguments for literacy bring to light a myriad of theoretical and experiential complications. From his earliest and perhaps most well-known book, *Pedagogy of the Oppressed* (translated into English in 1968), to his most recent collection of essays, Freire maintains his emphasis on the uneven alignment between the constituencies of third-world literacy. In *Pedagogy* he speaks of oppressors and invaders, the oppressed and the liberated. The oppressors he regards as subjects, the oppressed as objects. Indeed, a sign of the oppressed person's move away from oppression is an assumption of subjective status. Yet Freire also recognizes a middle ground in which former "objects" of oppression may themselves become "subject" oppressors. As he says in *Pedagogy* (all feminism aside), the oppressed desire to be men "but for them to be men is to be oppressors. This is their model of humanity" (30). An example is the phenomenon of peasant overseers who tyrannize their compatriots.

Yet theoretical and practical problems result from Freire's dichotomies: they hamper his ability to carry through his arguments for the importance of literacy. For Freire, the exigence of literacy is knowledge; literacy is knowledge making. He says that as illiterates become literate, they learn "to know in a different way what they knew before, but they also begin to know what before they did not know" (*Politics of Education* 162). Illiterates who become readers and writers become readers and writers of themselves as part of the world in which they live, as makers of the world and as victims of it. The point of literacy "is not properly speaking to fabricate the liberating idea but to invite the people to grasp with their minds the truth of their reality" (85). The truth of reality is often hidden within literacy, and literacy itself is hidden by the dominant classes who vest their interests in the continued mystery of unread words. Freire is not so foolish as to think that truth and reality reside within words themselves, but he speaks expressly of the process of "mythicization" of reality that occurs to keep literacy "opaque" and fragmented in the "innumerable alienating words and phrases" (49) that dominate education. The illiterates, at the hands of protectors, enjoy the status of marginal people. They are separated from life and presumably are in need of salvation. Like slum dwellers, they are "intrinsically wicked and inferior" (56). After all, Freire says, "it would be extremely naive to expect the dominant classes to develop a type of education that would enable subordinate classes to perceive social injustice critically" (102).

The alternative to the oppressive inculcation of literacy is an interrogation of literacy in which literacy rather than the illiterate becomes the object of question and in which one can "problematize" words (23). The result is "conscientization," the making sense of reality by piercing the myth of the irrationality whose agent is the written word. Conscientization occurs as people become literate and the mythology drops away. A Chilean peasant says:

> You can't imagine what it was like to go to Santiago to buy parts. I couldn't get oriented. I was afraid of everything— afraid of the big city, of buying the wrong thing, of being cheated. Now it's all different. (60)

The resulting enlightenment requires a constant struggle against the internalization of dominant values. Freire describes, for example, a "semi-intransitive" state of consciousness in which new literates interiorize the "dominator's style of life" (53). This occurs because peasants have lived under domination for so long. According to Freire,

> to the extent . . . that the interiorization of the dominator's values is not only an individual phenomenon but also a social

and cultural one, ejection must be achieved by a type of cultural action in which culture negates culture. That is, culture
as an interiorized product that in turn conditions men's subsequent acts must become the object of men's knowledge so
that they can perceive its conditioning power. (43)

The "residue" of cultural myths implicit in the lives of people
who have long been denied social control is not easily wiped
away.

Freire understands that interiorization of oppression is profound. Populist leaders, for whom Freire has measured use,
often degenerate into manipulators who manipulate "the
masses since [they] cannot manipulate the elite" (78). More
insidious is the manipulative elite, often goodhearted people
who see themselves as experts who turn literacy into a "spe-
cialism." Of specialists, Freire says, "Because they have lost
the vision of the whole of which their speciality is only one
dimension, they cannot even think correctly in their specialty"
(88). Humanitarian teachers, newly literate peasants, populist
leaders, the very downtrodden who behave in a "prescribed"
manner—all contribute to the oppression of massive numbers
of people (31).

Freire's significant contribution to understanding this situation is his delineation of the economic dualities of literacy. He
is willing to acknowledge that his own understanding is subject
to revision. As he says of apparent clashes between teachers
and students, philosophy and pragmatics,

> that is why reflection is only legitimate when it sends us back
> ... to the concrete context where it seeks to clarify the
> facts. . . . In throwing light on an accomplished action, or one
> that is being accomplished, authentic reflection clarifies
> future action, which in its given time will have to be open to
> renewed reflection. (153)

Yet Freire's most pressing dilemma is still with us. How,
in his words, can "the oppressed, as divided, unauthentic
beings," participate in developing the pedagogy of their "liberation" (Pedagogy 33). His answer is dramatic but arbitrary:
students and teachers of literacy must assume "a radical posture," a posture of solidarity. The pertinent question for us
concerns the literacy connection within the debate about the
constitution of the human profile. A widely given answer is
that literacy confers special power, the power to be human. To
be wanting in literacy is to be wanting in human fulfillment.

But literacy is more than self-fulfillment. Literacy is also social and political and economic in nature. Society wields its literacy more powerfully than the individual and a fight against the literate bureaucracy is more than, say, a fight against City Hall. Literacy neither imprisons nor frees people; it merely embodies the enormous complexities of how and why some people live comfortably and others do not.

George Dennison, in *The Lives of Children*, describes a young student stymied by literacy: the student attends a school for "incorrigible" elementary students. Dennison writes of Jose:

> When I used to sit beside Jose and watch him struggling with printed words, I was always struck by the fact that he had such difficulty in even seeing them. I knew from medical reports that his eyes were all right. It was clear that his physical difficulties were the sign of a terrible conflict. On the one hand he did not want to see the words, did not want to focus his eyes on them, bend his head to them, and hold his head in place. On the other hand he wanted to learn to read . . . and so he forced himself to perform these actions. But the conflict was visible. It was as if a barrier of smoked glass had been interposed between himself and the words: he moved his head here and there, squinted, widened his eyes, passed his hand across his forehead. The barrier, of course, consisted of the chronic emotions I have already mentioned: resentment, shame, self-contempt, etc. But how does one remove such a barrier? (81)

Dennison sees a child who is battered by literacy and who shows it in every visible way, and he surmises that visibility is only the surface issue. He is right.

Dennison's example reminds us of the connections and the disassociations between literacy scholarship and ideas of the subjective world, especially the subjective world of the illiterate. Unfortunately, there is little useful scholarly work that speaks directly to the relationship between literacy and subjective life. The great division often proposed is between orality and literacy; the premise is that oral language promotes dramatically, intrinsically different lives and societies than do reading and writing. Yet notions of orality seem curiously facile. Much is made of the value of facial expression, the temporal, the fleeting predisposition of oral language to disappear, and the facility of question-and-answer episodes. Oral discourse is presumed to deal in pure, committed, and dynamic meanings. If a speaker is unclear, the oral circumstance allows for clarity, indeed, demands it. Romanticized or sanitized interpretations result.

George Steiner supplies an example. In a popular publication, he begins an address about the "Future of Reading" by disclaiming a future. He says, "It is hardly necessary . . . to cite all the evidence of the depressing state of literacy" ("Books" 21). Steiner grieves the loss of "reading in the old, private, silent sense" and suspects dangerous consequences of the loss. He tells the story of Erasmus, who picks up a scrap of print out of the mud: "As he bent to pick it up, he muttered a cry of joy, overcome by the wonder of the book, by the sheer miracle of what lies behind picking up such a message" (21). As for today, Steiner warns,

> in a vast traffic jam on a highway or in a Manhattan grid, we can insert a cassette of the Missa Solemnis into a tape deck. We can, via paperbacks and soon cable vision, demand, command, and compel the world's greatest, most existent, most tragic or delightful literature to be served up for us, packaged and cellophaned for immediacy. These are great luxuries. But it is not certain that they really help in the constant, renewed miracle that is the encounter with the book. (24)

Literacy is, to some extent, private and solitary, but the magical nature of Steiner's connections is too pat as well as overly romanticized. If Erasmus can find pleasure in a surprise message in the dirt, cannot a reader of computer bulletin boards find a similar pleasure? Yet Steiner's reverence for the spiritualism of the text is shared by many.

Of course, as romantic as turning pages may seem to the reader or writer who has time to do so, the argument for technology involves suppositions about the structures of thinking that literates demonstrate. In this respect, questions of cognition become more or less transformed into questions about memory, right- or left-brain capabilities, or motor coordination. Disciplines devoted to the study of literacy from this perspective tend to speak of the "cognitive structure" or of the "thinking process." Much effort is devoted to drawing maps of cognitive reality, a reality reflected within either the text or the behavior of the reader/writer. In these cases, however, the researchers make a leap between the cognitive models they formulate out of boxes and arrows and the way the models relate to the literate person.

Mike Rose's work on writer's block provides a useful example. Rose sets out six cognitive and dysfunctional dimensions of writer's block. These dimensions include premature editing, poor planning, and so forth (4–7). Rose conceptualizes a "schematic representation of selected cognitive dimensions and functions of the composing process." This representation places at the top of the cognitive project "Executive Operations," and at the bottom, "Task Environment" with two-way arrows in between. "Executive Operations" are threefold: "high level strategies (usually based on assumptions), goals, problem-solving/composing styles." Lateral operations in the schema consist of the "Composing Subprocesses," which themselves consist of diverse components such as rules in one box and knowledge in another (12). Rose attributes much of his model building to Flower and Hayes, whose "process model" of writing also depicts a number of boxes that writers negotiate arrow by arrow.

Rose and others who focus on cognitive structure draw upon Noam Chomsky and other linguistic structuralists. According to these scholars, the structures of the brain, or the part of the brain that handles language, may be understood as distinct from other aspects of a self/subject and can also be assumed to exist universally. To wit, everyone learns to speak, so everyone must possess the deeply ingrained capacity to do so. Unfortunately, the cognitive approach to literacy begs central questions. Compartmentalizing people's brains into different kinds of memories or sensitivities boils back down to ideology. At best, as Rose shows in a few of his case studies of cognitively blocked writers, there may be covariance between a quotation mark that is confidently inscribed and a quotation mark that is correctly used (83). However, it would appear quite difficult to describe the structure of confidence in being a good grammarian as a grammatical artifact of the structure of correct quotation marks.

Less "scientistic" in approach are Luria and Vygotsky, yet they remain committed to perceptual structures. Vygotsky's notion of "inner speech" postulates a relationship between a child (a language acquirer) and a child's world whose bridge to the adult world is language. Susan Wells, in "Vygotsky Reads Capital," likens Vygotsky's distinctions among stages of speaking (thinking) to Marx's analysis of the relationships among commodities. Both scholars, she says, seem "interested in analyzing the relationship among the basic elements of a concept rather than in narrating its concrete development." The narration of concrete development, however, is the primary interest of many literacy theorists as they try to turn a particular literacy event into an imprint of structural development. Within the broader cognitive range, the question confuses reality with the mind. Minds are presumed to effect a reality, literacy a part of that reality, the literate mind effecting unique realities. Hence, the conceptual worlds brought forth by the literate and the illiterate are ineluctably different.

The research, indeed, suggests that literates have different structures of mind and reality from illiterates. Frank D'Angelo's *Conceptual Theory of Rhetoric* attempts to describe, for example, two literate structures, or strategies, for effecting meaning, i.e., making sense of a text. In one of his essays on the connection between mind and literacy, D'Angelo summarizes the popularly held distinctions between illiterate and literate mind structures. Basing the summary on a study of Luria, he says:

> [I]n contrast to the kinds of abstract, conceptual thinking found in literate people, the kinds of thinking associated with nonliterate people is concrete and specific, embedded in the particular situation. Such thinking tends more toward the sensorimotor and perceptual rather than the conceptual. Once, however, literacy is acquired, the way the individual perceives reality undergoes radical restructuring. . . . There is a dramatic transition from sensorimotor and perceptual thinking to propositional thinking. The thinking of nonliterate people, however, evidently does not advance beyond the level of what Piaget calls the stage of concrete operations. ("Luria on Literacy" 155)

This description is a statement of the humanist position about the technological effects of literacy; it might be noted that similar descriptions have been made about college-level "basic writers" in the United States, students who appear to lack the ability to conceptualize because their writing skills are not up to par with a general freshman population (Lunsford, "Cognitive Development and the Basic Writer").

Of course, many hasten to add that illiterates are not inferior in intelligence. According to D'Angelo, some skills or knowledge may be better acquired without the services of literacy. But, on the whole, he says, "the ability to conceptualize and handle abstract symbols is absolutely necessary in a technological society" ("Luria on Literacy" 168). Not to avail these skills is tantamount to perpetrating "hopeless deprivation" in the lives of many citizens ("Luria on Literacy" 168). Indeed, if nonliterates can be taught to conceptualize, according to the D'Angelo scenario, the problems of illiterate life will be solved. This would be fine unless one asks why literacy inspires the literate while the illiterates toil in their own ineffectual devices?

At blame for some of these conceptions is an oversimplified or underappreciated idea of self, not to mention the social context of individual life. Two literacy theorists who attempt to make sense of this idea, and who openly acknowledge the subject/object schism, are Walter Ong, an American Jesuit, and Keith Hoskin, a professor of Classics at the University of Warwick.

In "Reading, Technology, and Human Consciousness," Ong says that literacy presents a qualitatively different situation from almost any other human scene:

> Writing and reading establish a special situation marked by absences, gaps, silences, and opacity. Faced with a text, readers find that both the author and original context are absent. Readers themselves have to produce an equivalent of both— the equivalent, for they produce neither author nor context in total actuality. The context is no more, and the author, often enough, is dead. (173)

Ong's apparent trust in the transparency of an "actual" context is rather naive, of course, and even the New Critics proffered more sophisticated arguments concerning an author's ability, dead or alive, to supply answers to the total meaning of the total context in which a literacy event exists. Also, Ong assumes the simplicities of face-to-face communication, which presume that speakers conduct more meaningful, clear interchange because they are in each other's bodily presence.

Nonetheless, Ong elucidates the relationships that texts presuppose. To interpret a text means, he says, "inserting it somehow into the ongoing conversations you live with" (174). At the same time, he understands that part of the difficulty of interpretation stems from the textuality of the relationship itself. Indeed, he believes that "Texts exist in relation to other texts much more than in relation to spoken language" (176). This is to say, as he puts it, that texts are never preterit yet are never autonomous, either. In fact, it is the interiority of the textual relation that singularizes it. Thus, Ong believes that the act of reading and writing can be construed as nothing less than "a stage in the evolution of human consciousness, that is, in the evolution of mankind's way of relating the human, the human interior world . . . " (179).

The technology of literacy, therefore, provides a singular, one might say insular, phenomenon. Its effect is to set off a central, perhaps cataclysmic, certainly psychic, shift in human destiny. Ong describes such a shift repeatedly: "Without writing and print the interiorization of consciousness that marks modern man could not have taken place" (181). Again, "Of all forms of verbal communication, chorographic and typographic communication—the use of writing and print—is in many ways the most deeply interiorizing" (183). Again:

> Writing entail[s] both the death of the old orality and the realization of previously hidden potentials of the word. There can be no doubt that for the advance of human consciousness, for its greater actualization, writing and reading, with the interiorization they implement and enforce, have been indispensable, absolutely required. (185)

What is the nature and genesis of this interiorization that human consciousness has undertaken? For Ong, part of the answer is spiritual. Any creature who can say *I*, Ong believes, is an interior being (179–180). Such is the de facto argument of human/language links. A second part of this interiority concerns silence, privacy, decontextualization—all of the technologically availed circumstances that distinguish literacy from orality. A third part of the interiority argument, however, and the part that is most suggestive but not elaborated by Ong (who appears to be caught up in exploration of the first two aspects of literacy), concerns the peculiar inhabitation of literacy. The technology of writing down and reading from, mixed with other intellectual abilities and other technologies, seems to produce different or new interiors.

Coercive literacy is perhaps too strong a descriptor for Ong, yet his mission is to advance the idea of intervention between technology and the user of it. Far from displacing orality, literacy reinforces it; "at the same time [it] utterly transforms" other technologies of communication,

> technologies within human consciousness. . . . Once the mind has become familiar with extensive analytic thinking through the use of writing, it becomes possible to proceed orally to some degree in analytic fashion. (188)

The notion suffers from familiar overstatement. *Analytic thinking is not a product of writing.* On the other hand, one cannot simply ignore the force of a technology that enters into lives with such repetition and abundance as literacy and expect its presence not to be felt. The problem Ong encounters, thus, is not with the difficulty of the literacy/human interaction, for that difficulty can hardly be overemphasized. Ong's problem, in fact, is that he settles for oversimplification. Given the notion that the technology of literacy affects thinking and that thinking affects technology, Ong colors the affair with a glossy sheen. Technology whirs its messages to people, and people from the bottom of their oral origins reply and change the technology for the better.

In Ong's words:

> Man and machine are more intimately related than most persons think, but in no simple way. In the perspectives being developed here, we must keep in mind that when technology is interiorized through writing and print and electronics, man does not by that simple fact become mechanized. Rather, when technology is interiorized, machines are humanized. Technology not only transforms consciousness and noetic processes but is itself transformed by consciousness. (191)

Whereas Ong makes a determined effort to bridge the duality between technology and the human subject, he undermines the effort with a benign conception of both technology and human purpose.

It is difficult to understand the humanization, the spiritualization, of a machine. The concept is difficult enough when confined to industrial contexts; the transformation from labor intensive to information technology makes the shift even more problematic. Most machines, from fast-food dispensers to corrugated laminators, appear unsympathetic to human modes of production, or distribution, or consumption. It is worth recalling Marcuse on this point. With a bluntness born of the apprehension of technology, Marcuse says:

> In the face of the totalitarian features of this society, the traditional notion of the "neutrality" of technology can no longer be maintained. Technology as such cannot be isolated from the use to which it is put; the technological society is a system of domination which operates already in the concept and construction of techniques. (xvi)

In other words, neither technology nor the human inventor is innocent. Can the technology of text change the course of human thinking? If it can, is literacy a machine? If it is necessary, what (and how) does text yield such power? And, finally, why, as this analysis has suggested, is that power violent?

Ong puts his faith in an evolutionary demand of consciousness to interiorize itself via the exteriorization of print. Keith Hoskin offers another approach to these questions. He suggests a technological transformation abetted by the technology of literacy but rooted in historical demand. The value of Hoskin is that he makes no bones about the powerfulness of the literate technology and the social source that wields it. He says, for example, that "the history of education is the history of writing; such is the programmatic statement I wish here to investigate" ("History of Education" 1). At the same time, he claims that writing comes about historically and institutionally as a means to control, to index, to "double-text" the society. As he says, "If I am right ... a highly significant moment [is] when writing re-writes itself and discovers a new power as examination, discipline, and control ... " ("Cobwebs to Catch Flies" 4).

Hoskin's argument is complex, broad, and well documented with historical example. He describes the instances of the introduction and eventuation of writing within the history of Western society in order to show how the technique becomes an artifact, an artifact the beginnings of an institution, an institution the enforcement of surveillance and standardization. Hoskin shows, for example, how the definition of "learning" changes in postalphabetic Greece to distinguish between teaching and learning; originally the Greek word implied no distinction; the change accommodated ideas of successful, authoritative teaching despite student failure to learn. Hoskin shows how forgeries in eleventh-century Rome begot a system of dating and multiple copying by the thirteenth century, and he traces the adoption by Cambridge University in the eighteenth century of a system of written examinations in order to weed out deviants who had not acquired the proper competences. These competences then became set curricula. For Hoskin,

> written performance becomes a record or archive of the individual; it begins to be given a mathematical "mark," the marks form a distribution, and the individuals a "population"

> of subjects objectively known through their possession of
> quantified attributes. ... ("Cobwebs" 13; also "The Examina-
> tion" 144)

The history of writing is a history of examination.

Thus, Hoskin traces very good cases for the social aggran-
dizement of literacy. He repudiates the idea of "triumphant"
technology that Marshall McLuhan and Neil Postman advance,
observing that "new discourses may become possible but they
do not eventuate in a historic vacuum"; and he concerns himself with "regimes of truth" more than with ideas of "truth as
such" ("History of Education" 5, 15).

Unlike those who invest in the virtuous transcendance of
literacy, Hoskin finds the technology of Western literacy a rational contradiction. He sees the advent of literacy as a historical
reality with a suprahistorical potential: The "power/knowledge
significance of writing is transformed by the alphabetic break-
through." It is the invention of the alphabet that is the extraordinary achievement, and it is the repeatability of this invention
that holds the greatest fascination for Hoskin.

Hoskin concludes that the alphabet itself is an inverse her-
meneutic, a contradiction that contradicts itself and thereby
extends its power. The result is that the "theoretical structure
of the sign system" uses its "standardizing quality" to standardize ambiguity; the entire realm of communication, postalphabetic literacy, is permanently destabilized ("Cobwebs"
23). Thus, the definition of power as well as the usurpation and
maintenance of power, and all in between, depends on new
ways not merely of making literate rules but of interpreting
them. Autonomy, or power, comes to assume a double face: A
literate is able to go beyond mimesis, yet a literate is never
entirely understood. As Hoskin states, "Silent reading and writing remove the right to one's own voice even as they are apparently doing the opposite" ("Cobwebs" 13). The learning of
literacy is the submission to it, "to be shaped in certain ways"
by the "pedagogy of print" ("History of Education" 10).

As Hoskin says, literacy is a unique, apparently one-time
invention, and its uniqueness makes literacy a technology
unlike any other and, ironically, more indescribable. But literacy is not itself ineffable, and this is what Hoskin forgets. As
profound as the technology of literacy is, it is a technology. It is
an invention. Literacy, simply, is not natural, and much results
from this.

This current discussion began with questions about the synthesis between personal and social forces in the instance of literacy. As evidenced in the work of Freire, literacy appears to support contradictory alternatives; it offers liberation or imprisonment. Further, it assumes an intrepid, clandestine persona in its ability to coerce or colonize the consciousness of literates or those who would be so. Literacy changes lives. The question is about the process, however; how does the change proceed? Is the head invaded by literate capabilities? Is human history rewritten by a magical pen? Or do individuals rewrite the course of human history only because they can write? As crude or broad as these questions may sound, they have not been disposed of. They are questions of human history as well as questions of contemporary education, and they involve literacy from its inception to the present day. When one asks about human history in this way, however, one asks how literacy is human. The only sure answer is that literacy does not know. It is odd to think that it might. Yet this notion of an autonomous force called literacy is precisely the concept Hoskin and others fall prey to.

There is no simple avenue into these issues. The assumptions of an autonomous literacy rest on presumptions about orality. These presumptions dichotomize orality and literacy and attribute widely divergent, and dangerous, features to each. Orality is presumed to indicate tidier instances of verbal communication and more forthright needs to communicate at all. Yet autonomous literacy presumes both simplistic orality and complex literacy.

Eric Havelock makes more clear the strains of power literacy heard in Hoskin, Ong, Vygotsky, and others. Whereas Hoskin tinkers with the nuance of alphabet, Havelock enshrines it. In "The Alphabetization of Homer" he describes the "original act" of literacy as

> something like a thunderclap in human history, which our bias of familiarity has converted into the rustle of papers on a desk. It constituted an intrusion into culture, with results that proved irreversible. (3)

He continues, "It laid the basis for the destruction of the oral way of life and the oral modes of thought" (3).

Havelock conceives the development of literacy as an oddly stultifying yet mobilizing phenomenon in the history of consciousness, the force of literacy veritably coming up against itself to form postliterate forms of thought. He says that

> as documentation takes place, a restless, moving sea of words becomes frozen into immobility. Each self-contained moment of recitation . . . becomes imprisoned in an order no longer acoustic but visible. It ceases to be a soundtrack and becomes almost an intangible object. A collocation of such objects takes place as they are gathered and written. Because they are now preserved outside the individual memories of those who inscribe and gather them, the gatherer need no longer surrender himself totally and temporarily to absorption in any of them. He is able to look at them in the mass and become aware of them as a sum, a totality. As he does this he begins to wake up from the dream. (18)

The dream?

The encomium of the dream catches one short. The themes of literacy have been rumbling under the surface of peroration, but now they come together, all of a claim. Havelock turns the theoretical pining after literacy into a daily, routine metaphor. There is a difference between literate and nonliterate life. The nonliterate lives in a dream, in a world of make-believe, in a state of "total absorption." The literate, on the other hand, actually lives. It must be emphasized that Havelock is not endorsing cultural relativity. He is voicing the fundamental claim for the power of literacy, which explains, he believes, not merely postliterate history but preliterate as well—explains, demarcates, and evaluates. The thing to understand about literacy, he says, is that it makes minds. He is bolder. Literacy makes minds intelligent.

Havelock's argument has rested on a comparative analysis of two alphabets, one good, one bad. The bad one is cuneiform; the good one is the linear Greek alphabet. Havelock studies two passages in the two alphabets, passages about the great flood. He counts the number of repetitive words in each passage. He discovers that the cuneiform users, the Mesopotamians, repeated themselves more often than the Greeks. He decides that this is because they had recourse to fewer words they could write down. This is because they had an alphabet that could not be shaped to innumerable ideas—unlike the Greek alphabet. The consequence of this is that the Mesopotamians, who may or may not have had rich ideas, could transmit only a certain number of them, and they were the ideas that could be accommodated by an incommodious alphabet (9).

Yet how is an untransmitted idea an idea? This is a dilemma for Havelock. He assumes that the powerfulness of a technology is prior to the genesis of ideas. As for communication, he says, "linguistic statements [can] be remembered and repeated only as they [are] specially shaped" (4). When language is solely spoken, it is the ears that do the shaping, according to Havelock. However, literacy brings to bear "an automatic marriage" between sound and symbol, the symbol system possessing "a unique phonetic efficiency" (4) that suits all needs. Sign systems thus encourage people to "pack" into language "the full variety of expression which . . . description calls for" (9). Unfortunately, "the deficiencies of cuneiform as an instrument of acoustic-visual recognition" discourage the composer from maximum packaging (9). Havelock concludes:

> We must presume, therefore, that behind the scribal [Mesopotamian] version of the flood, which is all we have, lies hidden forever, and lost to us forever, a far richer epic, which, obeying the law of cultural storage, performed for those cultures the functions that Homer performed for preliterate Greece. (9)

Even the spoken lingua of Mesopotamians was "probably less sophisticated," however. (9) The Mesopotamians apparently couldn't master rhyme any better than they could get all their thoughts on papyrus.

Despite the rather shrill tone of this argument, Havelock has the full weight of ideology and academic tradition behind him; he says what literates want to hear and he says it to the literates who have the most to gain. One need only think of the vast academic rationalizations about literacy that cause many to lose out to literacy—losers who fail to overcome an "oral" tradition in order to enter the more standard literate one. Indeed, Havelock's argument *is* the familiar rustle of paper on school desks. Those who shuffle the most papers from the front of the room will continue to control the direction of students' futures and to justify their right to do so through literacy. Certainly, Havelock does.

Havelock himself names the most readily apparent problem. His model of literacy, of comprehension of literacy, is one of transmission. He places his stock in a top-down, sending operation that presumes a crystallization of the "content" of spoken words and "precipitate[s] a deposit upon the bottom" (4). Thus, although it is easy for him to postulate the preexistence of ideas that may be lost forever to a deficient alphabet, he cannot articulate what those ideas might be like or what uses they might have served, unless the uses mirror the same ideas promulgated in Westernized alphabets.

We might also question whether orality is really so simple. Literacy is a complicated item, but are "oral thinkers" given to more consistent (persistent?), constrained ideas? A positive answer to these questions is the bedrock of Havelock and his colleagues' arguments. But are these differences real? Are oral subjectivities cut from a different cloth than literate? Certainly, this query can be chalked up with the rest of the superiority-from-literacy arguments. It is merely out of Western economic necessity that we presume not merely a difference but a natural hierarchy between oral and literate peoples. In this respect, we might look at a final example of the subjective sanction of literacy to attempt to understand how these collisions between individuals and literacy, literacy and history, history and human purpose occur. Where we have to begin, however, is at the point of human definition, where all literacy discussions automatically take their cue but rarely their voice.

A useful way to approach this point is through "wild child" cases in which, aside from other features, the subject is identified on the basis of absent or aberrant linguistic heritage. Such cases exist on the borders of disciplinary studies, but because they do, they clarify the boundaries. Of interest here is how the sociolinguistic perception and treatment of "wildness" inform our understanding of the relationship between literacy and humanity. As an example, let's focus on the case of Genie, whose story is told by Susan Curtiss, a teacher and researcher at the University of California, Los Angeles. It was largely through the efforts of Susan Curtiss that Genie learned language; of interest to Curtiss was Genie's ability to do so.

Before Genie was found, and Curtiss began working with her, she was imprisoned until age twelve in a room in her house, isolated from most persons except her father. Curtiss describes Genie's circumstances as follows:

> Hungry and forgotten, Genie would sometimes attempt to attract attention by making noise. Angered, her father would often beat her for doing so. In fact, there was a large piece of

wood left in the corner of Genie's room which her father used solely to beat her whenever she made any sound. During these times, and on all other occasions that her father dealt with Genie, he never spoke to her. Instead, he acted like a wild dog. He made barking sounds, he growled at her; and if he wished to merely threaten her with his presence, he stood outside the door and made his dog-like noises. . . . (6)

Genie was spotted by a social worker and was removed from the home. The father committed suicide. At the same time Genie was cared for socially she also became an experiment. The focus of the experiment was her process of acquiring language, measured against a battery of linguistic tests to discover the extent to which she could acquire language like other children. She was tested for her grammar, for her phonemes, for "simple negation," "simple modification (one adjective + noun)," and so forth. On the basis of the "Many, Most, Few, Fewest" test, Curtiss concluded that "Genie's performance indicates that she does not understand any of these qualifiers" (135). Curtiss thought Genie's bad mood at the time of the test accounted for the failure or perhaps she did not understand the questions.

Curtiss often experienced problems on these issues, for Genie was not easily motivated. Curtiss says pointedly in the beginning,

Testing [Genie] was often extremely problematic and difficult. Especially in the first year of my work with her, getting Genie to attend to the test and respond in a meaningful way was difficult. As time passed, however, both of us became more successful with one another and I learned better how to work around her moods, to motivate her, and to get her to perform. (38)

As badly as Genie took to testing, however, Curtiss decided that "in real-life situations, Genie appears to comprehend almost everything that is said to her" (142). Curtiss continues:

Genie's language is far from normal. . . . [However], over and above the specific similarities and differences that exist between Genie's language and the language of normal children, we must keep in mind that Genie's speech is rule-governed behavior, and that from a finite set of arbitrary linguistic elements she can and does create novel utterances that theoretically know no upper bound. These are the aspects of human language that separate it apart from all other animal communication systems. Therefore, abnormalities notwithstanding, in the most fundamental and critical respects, Genie has a language. (204)

And if Genie did not? How unlike normal children would Genie be? How much closer to other "animal communication systems" would she come, and what would that mean about Genie? Curtiss's conclusion that Genie has a language is a conclusion not merely about Genie's language but about the pedigree that language confers. Genie speaks in rule-governed ways; therefore, Genie is human. The question is why Genie was ever presumed to be other than human, as her name ironically implies from an inverse perspective, indeed, Havelock's noble perspective. If Genie really were suspected to be magical, would she require the "Many, Most, Few, Fewest" test?

It is clear in the situation of this wild child that the father is the inhuman creature, not Genie. It is clear that the important issue is not whether Genie can use language as normal children can or if she can acquire language after twelve mute years. The real issue is whether Genie can ever inhabit a world in which language users no longer abuse her. Language researchers, of course, do not abuse her as her father did. But one asks rather bleakly if there are not more productive ways to see human beings, especially human beings so obviously victimized, than to judge them against a language standard. Genie is not a black child denied reading skills because of "black dialect," but the two situations bear similarities. Remarkable is the immutable reverence with which the idea of language is treated; the standard of language persists as though there were no other standards. Language to literacy, orality to alphabet, are bare steps in the conceptual leap. The bottom line remains the subdividing of human beings, and the reality is that literacy is an exceedingly powerful way to maintain the separation.

The case of Genie's language and the example of Havelock's literacy share a common bond. The baseline against which Genie's linguistic ability is judged arises from the "ideal" (Chomskian) world of perfect speakers and circumstances, total clarity. The literacy of Havelock embraces purely literate ideas. In both systems, the language system is impervious, removed from social concerns, which is not to say that language never changes. Because language systems shape subjectivity, indeed, sponsor it, the difference between literate and illiterate sensibilities is seen as marked. What we should do,

Havelock would assert, is enrich. Nonliterates must be brought into fuller life. After all, well-formed subjectivities, like well-formed sentences, demonstrate adjustment.

There is another way to understand literacy, however, one that locates it within its social context, its social context changed by it. To approach that way, we might consider the example of Fernand Braudel, in his extraordinary survey, *Capitalism and Material Life 1400–1800*, in which he writes of the ways and technologies of past lives that both shape and elude present realities. In a chapter on houses, clothes, and fashion (the "codes" one might say of visible life), Braudel observes a dialectic between people and the constraints they face or live in as occupants of their own world. What he shows is that de jure is not de facto, whether the frame is made of housing or linguistic material. Limitation is not codified, even if it seems it should be. In "constrained" civil circumstances, he says,

> repetition was all the more natural as building material varied little and imposed certain limitations on every region. This does not mean, necessarily, that civilizations lived absolutely according to the restrictions imposed by stone, brick, wood, or earth. But these materials often did constitute long-lasting limitations. "It is lack of stone," a traveler noted, "that obliges [the Persians] to build walls and houses of earth." In fact, they were built of sun-dried bricks. "Rich people decorate the outside walls with a mixture of whitewash, Muscovy green and bricks, and gum which makes them look silvery." Nonetheless they were still unfired bricks, and geography explains why, though it does not explain everything. *Human beings also had a say in the matter.* [emphasis added] (193)

Building materials, in other words, affected the kinds of buildings people lived in, and still do. However, clay and soil do not a house make and they do not dictate that houses are shaped into squares or roofs into A-frames. As Braudel observes later, even after the frail tent could have been replaced, it was not— though when it was, the stability of housing affected the stability of lives in many ways (197). Alphabets and ideas, communications and the humans who communicate, might be viewed in similar ways. What we must do is to relocate discussions about literacy within discussions about communications and society, the same way discussions of brick and mud must become issues of access to housing, rich and poor dwellings, heated and unheated conditions.

Hoskin, for example, has only a short distance to go to make this alliance. He links the forgery in Roman documents with the appearance of literacy; the conclusions Hoskin draws are conclusions about literacy, "its own power-knowledge logic" ("History of Education" 15). Yet literacy is the minor point in the discussion; the crucial issue is the genesis of both the document and the forgery. Which Romans claimed the privilege to use and abuse the privilege of writing? And what were those consequences? Forgery surely was aided by literacy, but what situations required aid?

Discussions of literacy must include a consideration of the hospitable environment where literacy can flourish. Such a hospitable world is what many comfortable academics believe literacy has called forth. But, indeed, their reasoning must be backwards. The understanding of literacy is not itself universal, and our reasons to act as if it were are not either. Many of our reasons are conventional, often selfish, and always economic. At this time in Western, and American, history, many people do not have to think about living. The essentials are taken for granted. But living is always defined by those on the margin. Those on the inside keep away the margin's encroachment just as assiduously as those on the outside suffer from it. The difference is that some draw in to survive while others pay to keep the mere survivors out. This is to say that the purely "literate" people (whom many academics have in mind when they discuss literacy) are folks who have the time to contemplate their good luck. They live as word merchants, but since words are not things, their labor assumes a peculiar character.

Of course, academics are not solely to blame for advocating a mysterious argument about literacy that also happens to ratify their own existence. The issue is more complex. It begins, as this discussion has tried to show, in the separation of object and subject and in what happens to the definition of each within private domains. Yet the real question is not how subject and object are different but how they are alike.

Extensive discussion of literacy advances the importance of human subjectivity, human consciousness, to identify the essence of language written and read. But what if there is no subject? Or, put a bit more narrowly, what if there is no linguistic subject, no verbal individual or single linguistic consciousness—and, moreover, no linguistic consciousness made out of additive, individual privacies, to account for the effects of literacy? If what has been usually taken as a subject were an integration of social acts and histories, acts that are clearly material, what would this do to the ideas of the power of literacy and to the power of human beings? What have we if we replace the paradigm of subjective and objective literacy with material literacy?

Chapter Two dealt with the habit of treating literacy as a thing while expressing interest in its other (subjective) characteristics. The materiality of literacy is its hardware. This notion is mistaken, but from the mistake many consequences follow. We might look, for example, at the kind of advice literates give to people who would like to be so. In *Writing with Power*, a composition book for college students, Peter Elbow pleads with students to "clean up" their language with the goals of "precision and energy" in mind. He continues:

> The more you zero in on the precise meaning you have in mind, the more you can strip away unnecessary words and thereby energize your language. The key activity is crossing out words and sentences. Your new draft may have large chunks from your raw first-draft writing, rearranged with scissors and staples. These sections may need extensive cutting. (34)

Elbow perceives a veritable landscape, overgrown with staples and "unnecessary words"; his idea of the materiality of literacy recalls strip mining. Other weeders and scissors wielders advocate similar procedures to hack away lifeless, useless, "unenergized" literacy. The readability experts, such as Joseph Williams, regard word count as instrumental to perspicacity. "When we squeeze long, windy phrases into more compact phrases we make diffuse ideas sharply specific . . . (132). Williams, recalling Havelock, finds the shape of lives in sentences, "the constantly changing syntactic prisms that refract experience into its parts and order them in coherent ways" (117). E. D. Hirsch, operating on similar planes of vacuity, explains how to separate the teaching of literature from the teaching of writing because one is a breach of the other's antimaterial condition:

> The study of style in literature is a study of the fusion of form with content. But learning to write implies just the opposite assumption; it assumes the separation of linguistic form and content. Learning the craft of prose is learning to write the same meaning in different and more effective ways. (Hirsch 141)

For Hirsch, as with others, the materiality of literacy suggests language divorced from content and from social and economic realities.

The popular idea of material literacy is entirely compatible with academic perspectives. The August 1985 issue of *Harper's Magazine* devotes itself to the demise of the book. "Will books survive?" asks the lead article, and many publishers and editors and booksellers profess not to know. Bookstore owners say "our sales strategy today is to throw a bunch of books against the wall and see which ones stick." Publishers add,

> Our challenge is not just to edit valuable books . . . but somehow to get them out to the many booksellers who are unreceptive to them. Recently, a man who runs a big chain [said] with undisguised pride that 30 percent of the stock in his stores is nonbooks: audio cassettes, videotapes, posters, T-shirts, whatever. But we're in the book business. It's supposed to be our responsibility to get books out to people. ("Will Books Survive?" 42)

To be sure, book editors and publishers have unique reasons to value books with covers and pages in between; these items translate into dollars and cents. Yet this glazed view of literacy will do more harm than good for those who continue to plow their money into the idea of the supremacy of print.

The South Carolina Elections Commission in 1985 recommended that the state convert to electronic voting machines. The machines would replace a haphazard, often costly system of printed, dissimilar ballots. The plan was met with grave distrust by the Budget and Control Board. Said the treasurer of that Board, "I'm real squeamish about something I can't see. . . . " The treasurer was particularly concerned that "the only paper record would be a printout of composite vote totals." The treasurer was joined by other state officials, including the governor, who agreed that the idea may be sound but probably unaffordable even though the recommendation was based on the savings it would net for the state (Stracener C1). Certainly, the 1948 election of Lyndon Johnson to the United States Senate puts the lie to any method of literacy as insurance of law or fairness. Whatever the cost-effectiveness, this and other instances of material notions of literacy are not trivial, and they draw forceful reactions. Stanley Fish simply throws out the reality, i.e., the materiality, of print. "So once again," he says, in one of his many essays, "I have made the text disappear . . . " (173). According to Fish, since texts do not exist and only people do, then only people who communicate and interpret "textual" meanings in the same way can speak (or write) to one another. In fact, he says, communities of speakers/writers are built of old-boy networks, and this is how it should be:

> The only "proof" of membership [in a community] is fellow-ship, the nod of recognition from someone in the same community, someone who says to you what neither of us could prove to a third party: "we know." (173)

The status quo is Fish's ultimate achievement; so is the canon.

The real argument is not that texts, or print/literacy, do not exist or that they exist in the mind. That is the argument that a subjective paradigm dictates. On the other hand, to reduce text, the "stuff" of literacy, to mere stuff is not only insouciant but dangerous. Braudel, again, shows how not to bow to arbitrary, culture-limited ideas. He takes an object so presumably solid and obvious as a chair to show that its informing idea is sitting and that sitting is politic. In China, before the thirteenth century, he says, the height and placement of chairs accorded the status of people who sat in them. Moreover, there was "also a sort of division between seated life and squatting life at ground level, the latter domestic, the former official: the sovereign's throne, the mandarin's seat, benches and chairs in schools" (210). In other words, chairs are hardly mere objects in which one reclines or not, just as reclining is an evolutionary, as well as revolutionary, act.

In terms of literacy, there must be a similar view to its material existence. Not only has the material been confused with the physical, the physical itself has taken on mysterious, transcendental qualities. Literacy is taken to equal literacy from time beginning to end. This cannot be, however. Physically, a kind of literacy like a book may be used as a doorstop or as toilet paper. The point is that reading is not holding a text, writing is not moving a pencil or punching a keyboard, and voting is not X-ing a ballot. We have to stop acting as though they were.

Freire cannot resolve the dilemma of the subjective response to literacy because he, too, embraces idealism, the kind that fails to grasp the materiality of literacy and instead sees it as a physical object—a word or picture—or as a subjective (individual) abstraction. These are the same dualities with which he characterizes human relationships and, finally, the human individual (Shaull 12). If the mind is understood as the inscrutable ingredient in the process of liberation, and if to try to understand the mind is to believe it exists somewhere not here, then the result is to lose the connection between literacy and the world. What Freire and others need to locate is not the mind but the ideology of mind that undermines the connections. By locating that, they can move toward a philosophy of language that accounts for that ideology.

Such philosophies are not common, but V. K. Volosinov offers one approach that has promise not merely for its claims but for its willingness to ask the hard questions. "What, in fact, is the subject matter of the philosophy of language?" begins the search in Volosinov's single book, *Marxism and the Philosophy of Language.* "And where are we to find it?" A brief glimpse into Volosinov's investigations yields alternative locations. Though Volosinov devotes much of his efforts to resisting early twentieth-century Russian platforms of idealism, psychologism, and linguistics, his elaborations of the nature and force of language are remarkably salient for the current discussion of literacy; even the caveats that such a discussion requires pay tribute to the breadth of Volosinov's thought.

Volosinov is relentless in his attack on the relegation of important issues to the domain of "consciousness," a domain that he doubts not in fact but in kind and degree. For him, that which exists for human beings is that which exists between and among them, and this social contract constitutes both individual consciousness as well as social control. He frames the observation with an analogy:

> In order to observe the process of combustion, a substance must be placed in the air. In order to observe the phenomenon of language, both the producer and the receiver of sound and the sound itself must be placed into the social atmosphere. (46)

Volosinov directs his efforts to establishing the utter materiality of the word and its socioeconomic presence. In the final analysis, he refuses to give the word away, especially to itself. This keeps him at the forefront of all deliberations on language, but it especially places him counter to prevailing notions of the peculiar power of literate words.

Volosinov begins his exegesis of language with a critique of models of psychology because those models preempt a language as real as everyday life. In the late 1920s, he confronted an intellectual milieu of displacement: science threatened psychology and psychology undermined philosophy. With a view toward a third field, linguistics, Volosinov set about debunking the debates. In a statement concerning the mutual ineptitude of philosophy and psychology to handle their own claims about meaning, Volosinov says,

> Despite the deep methodological difference between them, the idealistic philosophy of culture and psychologistic cultural studies, both commit the same fundamental error. By localizing ideology in the consciousness, they transform the study of ideologies into a study of consciousness and its laws; it makes no difference whether this is done in transcendental or empirical-psychological terms. This error is responsible not only for methodological confusion regarding the interrelation of disparate fields of knowledge, but for a radical distortion of the very reality under study as well. (12)

This is to say that both philosophers and psychologists allow themselves the right to make up laws of their own disciplines, and when they get into trouble, they appeal to what cannot be known lawfully or cannot be observed empirically. Thus, while consciousness becomes the sine qua non of real meaning, it also becomes the excuse for not being able to ascertain it. Volosinov, again, minces few words:

> By and large, consciousness has become the asylum ignorantiae for all philosophical constructs [and, by extension, psychological]. It has been made the place where all unresolved problems, all objectively irreducible residues, are stored away. Instead of trying to find an objective definition of consciousness, thinkers have begun using it as a means for rendering all hard and fast objective definitions subjective and fluid. (13)

The result is ideological power, which Volosinov differentiates from ideological meaning.

The difference is important. It lies in a fundamental assumption by Volosinov about how meaning is made, which takes him into the field of linguistics. He explores meaning as it emerges from a system of signs, a world or realm of signs, which exists not so much apart from physical, physiological people but immediately with them. The thrust of the argument for literacy concerns the sign that Volosinov considers quintessential—the word. But first he must lay the basis for the reality of the sign or, to put it more accurately, for its materiality.

Volosinov describes a sign not as a physical object but as "an ideological product . . . not only itself part of a reality (natural or social)," but a "converted" phenomenon that "reflects and refracts outside of itself" (9). For him, signs, the reality outside of physical objects, are *almost* as real as unsigned objects—food and shelter, for example, which are materials irreducible in basic respects. The sign that every object can become becomes so by conversion. Whereas "a physical body equals itself, so to speak" (9), meaning requires that objects be transformed. "Without signs, there is no ideology" (9), he says, but he adds, "The domain of ideology coincides with the domain of signs. They equate with one another" (10) and they "occur in outer experience" (11). Indeed, Volosinov goes far to force studies of language to take up social relationships, for nowhere else can signs occur. He calls such mediation a social organization founded in "interindividual territory." Two extraordinary implications result.

The first is that the destruction of the individual consciousness is but the destruction of the prevailing concept of individuality. Volosinov by no means fails to appreciate notions of an inner individual, notions that include inner speech. Yet his revision of individual consciousness is sweeping: "The individual consciousness is a socioideological fact" (12). And Volosinov delineates the false polarities set up between the "individual" and the "social," a polarity that ultimately pits against each other ideas of the "social" versus the "natural" (34).

The second implication is as important. The personification of consciousness, of interreality, is the word. It is language. Volosinov is terse: "The word is the ideological phenomenon par excellence" (13). At some length:

> What is important about the word . . . is not so much its sign purity as its social ubiquity. The word is implicated in literally each and every act or contact between people—in collaboration on the job, in ideological exchanges, in the chance contacts of ordinary life, in political relationships, and so on. Countless ideological threads effect in the word. It stands to reason, then, that the word is the most sensitive index of social changes, and what is more, of changes still in the process of growth, still without definitive shape and not as yet

accommodated into already regularized and fully defined ideological systems. (19)

We speak to understand, we do not understand all that we say. What Volosinov points to are the ends of both. Those ends, he knows, are difficult but not inexplicable.

What he says of language he maintains of all human relations: "Each word, as we know, is a little arena for the clash and crisscrossing of differently oriented social accents. A word in the mouth of a particular individual person is a product of the living interaction of social forces" (41). Words and anything else that people notice that "enters the social purview of the group" come from one place. The sign "must be associated with the vital socioeconomic prerequisites of the particular group's existence; it must somehow, even if only obliquely, make context with the bases of the group's material life" (22).

An understanding of the generation of meaning will not come from looking at icons or appealing to subjective mysteries or individual psyches. Indeed, those postulates themselves will never be understood "until the problem of ideology is solved" (31). In the meantime, the agitated, exploited character of the exchange of words cannot be subverted; exchanges occur in milieus that admit many purposes, and any number of them can be reductive and deprecatory.

Said generally, language changes or emerges not via attention to language but according to the purposes of people in social relationships with one another (67). Where there is inequity in those relationships, there is inequity in language, and it is there for all the world to understand because it is on the outside. Volosinov:

> The very same thing that makes the ideological sign vital and mutable is . . . that which makes it a refracting and distorting medium. The ruling class strives to impart a supraclass, an eternal character to the ideological sign, to extinguish or drive inward the struggle between social value judgments which occur in it, to make the sign uniaccentual. (23)

Thus the tension of shifting economies, shifting accents.

The caveats to Volosinov are few and brief. The first is his hyperfocus on language as the finest medium of human communication. He is characteristically clear about this, calling the word "the purest and most sensitive medium of social intercourse" (14); "we do not see or feel an experience—we understand it" (36). One cannot help but take issue with such blanket deletion of nonlinguistic life or such a rigorous dichotomy between symbol and silence. Certainly the language that we speak and read and write makes up much of our lives, but is it all? Probably not. The second reservation is closely allied; it concerns not so much what Volosinov says as the implications of it. Volosinov values language so highly that he sees those who do not use words as lacking consciousness. He says,

> it is the word that constitutes the foundation, the skeleton of inner life. Were it to be deprived of the word, the psyche would shrink to an extreme degree; deprived of all other expressive activities, it would die out altogether. (29)

For Volosinov, the psyche is the inner word, with attendant complexities and possibilities, above all social. No word is no psyche.

Despite these reservations, we can appreciate Volosinov's major accomplishment, his understanding of what is manifest by knowing and his challenge to the ideology that sees consciousness as separate from social context. In *Existentialism and Human Emotion*, Jean-Paul Sartre explains that antisocial ideology. "What people would like," he says, "is that a coward or a hero be born that way" (34). Against that ideology, Volosinov works feverishly. The new psychology, the new linguistics, the new biology (genetics) collude, in his view, to dehumanize members of society. They do it by privatizing the mind so that people are held entirely responsible for their actions or are entirely subjected to them, in either case entirely controllable by more powerful sources as a matter of necessity. Volosinov's counterposition of a dialectic between psyche and ideology, "a continuous dialectical interplay," ensures mutual obliteration as each becomes comprehensible (39). Volosinov's greatest claim is that the psyche is never alone or singly formed.

The answer to the questions of delineated humanity can be thus described: lives are defined by language if language is a tool of oppression. What Volosinov knew of language is surely true of literacy: the society that fixes the worth of speakers fixes the worth of their words also. If, as Sartre said on another occasion, hell is other people, then literacy is hell. One simply cannot ignore the fact of hellish literacy in numbers of lives, not those necessarily completely deprived of it (of which there are relatively few in Western countries) but those impoverished by an enterprising economy. We are thus thrown back onto the society to understand how literacy elaborates social relations. We can see that a theory of literacy must arise from the situations that call it forth. That those situations often do violence to the lives and opportunities of groups of people should be clear.

Another version of the violence of literacy is explored by Mark Poster, who is most concerned with the possibilities of surveillance permitted by our computerized ability to collect vast amounts of data. Collection and storage of data seem to occur in spite of usual forms of communication and unimpeded by them. Enormous amounts of information can be collected about individual people, groups, businesses—in ways and with capacities inhuman or, perhaps, extrahuman. He calls this information "dead knowledge" (*Foucault* 166). The point we might wish to make here, however, recalls earlier divisions of labor remarked by the Lynds—in a capitalist economy, people have always acted on one another. Now, these relations are simply more open to view; indeed, an "information machine" may cement old relations rather than bulldoze them. What disturbs Poster more than this, perhaps, is that those who control now have more ease to do so. These data-gathering machines monitor welfare payments, Medicare payments, criminality, credit, and so forth. Never before in our history have we had at our disposal the means to economize people as we do now.

A book, a text, a school literacy assignment, a word-processing job in which an operator inputs information all day are all circumstances fraught with the historical displacement of literacy. Who gives the assignment, about what subjects, and to what ends? These questions inhabit the situations that literacy inhabits. The situations are themselves sets of relationships; literacy, at most, can only regulate relationships. This cannot be said too strongly. The ways of literacy are reproductive of the material relationships of people, not the psyches of people. When and if literacy affects the psyche, the effect is fleeting, in both a historical and a developmental sense. Literacy is not a religious conversion. Indeed, if the moment of literacy produces some sort of psychical change, that change is a result of social forces, not literacy itself. The "psychic" situation of a ten-year-old who reads at a "second-grade level" is that of a child who has been denounced by a literate society.

Literacy, like communication, is a matter of access, a matter of opportunity, a matter of economic security—a total matter. The violence of literacy is the violence of the milieu it comes from, promises, recapitulates. It is attached inextricably to the world of food, shelter, and human equality. When literacy harbors violence, the society harbors violence. To elucidate the violence of literacy is to understand the distance it forces between people and the possibilities for their lives. To see this is to see how daily work proceeds, one worker related to another, axes of literacy drawing structures of alienation.

It is precisely the social dimension that is denied by many literacy theorists. Even those who go beyond the superficialities of literacy seem to deny what they know to be true. Jay Robinson, for example, hesitates not at all to label English teachers the harbingers of American literacy, "mandarins of print culture" ("What Is Literacy?" 3). At the same time he advocates mechanisms of literacy that not only spur mandarinism but exonerate it. Of the literacy testing of students, for example, for whom the results mean "economic if not physical survival," Robinson says, "To base entrance and licensure examinations on literacy is both inevitable and legitimate, for ours is a society that requires facility with the written word in almost all of its workaday activities" (2). Americans, Robinson implies, are just born literate by nationality. And who would change a nation?

Of course, elsewhere Robinson says that the aim of writing programs should be to help students "to develop as ethnographers of thought" ("Literacy in the Department of English" 492). He speaks bluntly and correctly of teachers' "own separately lived lives and our all-too-often separate social identities, our ways of being in a world that we did not necessarily choose" (492). But Robinson needs, also, to speak so clearly of the worth of those long untaught. He needs to say that our work is not to teach people the ways of literacy that already distance them from the ways of equality but to teach them to change the ways, to teach them to revise the society that impoverished and denied them from the beginning. Robinson may be correct when he predicts that some current mandarins of print will lose out to the "electronification of the word" and more will have to learn new ways to "hold onto that power" ("What Is Literacy?" 3). But do we really think that the introduction of computers and word processors into classrooms (especially "English" classrooms) and businesses will introduce new opportunities for those previously denied opportunity? Will the long disfranchised suddenly be transformed into the computer literate, and will the teachers who for so long ensured the success of certain groups of students at the expense of others reverse the process?

There is no reason to expect this. Is this reason to abandon literacy? There is reason for despair as we view much of the current literacy scholarship, but that is not to say that literacy should be abandoned. What we need to abandon are literacy practices that make unnatural and unfair the lives of human beings. Certainly, literacy signifies profound human communication. Yet literacy itself has nothing to say. What we must develop is an agenda for fair things to say and fair places to say them. These places are everywhere in our lives; they are especially in school, where much of our lives is spent. In schools and in other literacy programs, we can foster a literacy that fosters change.

To do this, we must remember who we really are. We are not just private individuals in whose private minds the printed word works powerful deeds. We are, to be sure, natural individuals, but we are social before we are born, and the commerce we do with literacy is always, fundamentally, social. We are arranged by our relations to literacy, to how and why literacy is produced, and to the effects of what literacy is about. The extension of these relations describes how close to the edge of survival we live.

CHAPTER FOUR

THE VIOLENCE
OF LITERACY

◆

What to do? What to do?

June Jordan is an acclaimed educator. She teaches in a college English department. She writes poetry. She writes essays. She writes children's stories. Black, female, and politically aware, she tackles issues of race, gender, and politics. She gave the keynote address to the 1982 meeting of the National Council of Teachers of English (NCTE) in Washington, DC. The title of her address was "Problems of Language in a Democratic State."

What to do? What to do? Jordan asked, about English education in America.

English education in America, Jordan said, is trouble. English education acts as gatekeeper. English education closes down opportunities, especially for minorities and untraditional students. English education narrows rather than opens the possibilities of social meaning and social action. English education should stop doing this, she said.

And so she proposed a plan to explode the curriculum and content of English courses. She planned to include and embrace the outside world in the subject of English, and to bring the broad offerings of an English activism to all courses throughout the educational system. To her mind, doing this will create a fairer and better society in which fairer and better English education plays a major part. She claimed that English teachers have the power to change the lives of their students (NCTE speech). In her own English courses, Jordan changes lives (*Harvard Education Review*). Jordan was eloquent. Her address was moving.

Immediately following Jordan, William Irmscher, the incoming president of the NCTE, spoke. Irmscher quickly dispatched Jordan. The leader of the largest English organization in the country had no use for tough ideas: "[If we] politicize this organization beyond its educational purposes, we will polarize the membership." If the organization confronts issues of "apartheid in South Africa, abortion and nuclear freeze" the organization threatens the "substance of English studies. If we are linked to almost everything, where do we terminate our chain of active concerns?" (54–56).

Irmscher concluded. "We must preserve the integrity of the profession" (56).

End of the final address at the 1982 NCTE. Given the relative statuses of Jordan and Irmscher in the hierarchy of the English profession, it is not surprising that six years later Michael Holzman writes of English teaching, "we should stop doing harm if we can help it." (138). Holzman's words are haunted by Mina Shaughnessy's words written ten years earlier:

> When one considers the damage that has been done to students in the name of correct writing, [any] effort to redefine error so as to exclude most of the forms that give students trouble in school and to assert the legitimacy of other kinds of English is understandable. (9)

The 1988 address for the closing General Session at NCTE was given by Shirley Brice Heath. The title was, "Will the Schools Survive?" She claimed that schools would survive. She quoted Adrienne Rich to say that the schools might "reconstitute the world." On the way to her conclusion, she contrasted the most cited disciplinary problems in the schools today with those of 1940. In 1940, the top problem was talking. Talking was followed by chewing gum, running in the halls, littering, making noise. These were 1940s problems. The problems of the 1980s began with rape, robbery, and assault. They dwindled to burglary, arson, bombings and murder, abortion, alcohol abuse, and vandalism (3). No 1940s problems were mentioned. The evidence hardly suggests optimism. Damage is more to the point.

The reality that Heath did not pursue—but that Irmscher before her excused—is the mendacity of comparing the education of the 1940s and the education of the 1980s. Rape, robbery, and bombings are not simply 1980s events: rape, robbery, and bombings simply permeate today's middle class and middle class schoolrooms. The fact is that these problems have always existed. They existed in the education of the poor and the weak, not because the (segregated) education itself was poor and weak but because the world in which such education existed was violent and exploitive. Education never has been separated from violence, from the outside. It is the outside that the middle class has kept at bay. Despite Heath's efforts and optimism, despite Jordan's militancy, despite Holzman's and Shaughnessy's terseness, it still does.

To see this is neither easy nor popular. To see why is what this chapter is about. It would be nice to say, "Look around you, look in your classes to see who is not there, look at the small, impoverished children and teenage mothers and calculate how many of them are destined for comfortable lives (not to mention professions), and then draw the conclusions." Indeed, many teachers already do this, and what teachers see and do—and what they would like to do—would probably provide more insight and more direction than 99 percent of academic writing.

To view the picture accurately, we have to address realities that often appear disparate and that rarely enter formal English discussions. We have to forbear clear connections to understand how we may not have seen clear connections before. Perhaps it is most comfortable to begin with something we know about, something that many of us may be familiar with but are confused or frustrated by, but something that is certainly on everyone's agenda. That something is *literacy*.

Literacy has, arguably, replaced English as the chief descriptor of what we are about—or what we are supposed to be about. English and Literacy—the pairing of these words—is not necessarily comfortable. A major difference between the two is that the results of endeavors in literacy are empirically documented, whereas the results of "work" in English are not. This is not a particularly good situation. As we will see, the documention of literacy is about as perverse as the lack of documention in English is peculiar. Perhaps to see—or to resee—the attempts to categorize literacy—or illiteracy—will facilitate an entry into broader issues that impact all of us but whose force differs according to our locations within and without larger systems of education. To this end, we might look first at the claims and results of literacy efforts in this country.

Because literacy programs often fail, much of the data is evidence of failure. Among other things, literacy programs fail to identify a populace, they fail to make literate the populace they encounter, and they fail to examine their failure. The curiosity is that, like English departments, literacy programs bear no responsibility for their failure. The distinction is that literacy programs, unlike English programs, do not hide their failure.

Most service programs purport to have a clientele. Demographic descriptions of that clientele usually describe people who need services. Literacy programs, however, cannot even grasp the numbers of people who might fit the profile. The overdetermination of the number of illiterates, for example, is extraordinary. Hunter and Harman hazard a populace of illiterates "from 23 million to 65 million" (ix). Frank Gaik summarizes several counts to conclude that at least 46 million Americans cannot perform "basic literacy tasks as citizens and consumers" (3). Jonathan Kozol, in *Illiterate America*, says that "57 million . . . can't fulfill basic tasks," and he cites claims that 75 to 78 million "can't read well enough to function" (9). Kozol claims that one in three adult Americans is illiterate. Who is on the block here? Fifty-seven million is a far cry from twenty-three million.

A similar range of estimates characterizes the data on the number of illiterate "clients" who are served by literacy programs. The Adult Basic Education agency targets 70 million and enrolls 20 million. Of the enrollees, in 1981, 8.9 percent earned the General Equivalency Diploma, 2.4 percent earned a diploma equivalency, and 50 percent dropped out (Gaik 9). Hunter and Harman say that in 1976 only 9 percent of the enrollees in Adult Basic Education programs earned eighth-grade certificates (67). Laubach Volunteers and the Literacy Volunteers of America reach 70,000 a year of the 60 to 70 million cited by Kozol (Kozol 40–43).

A concomitant of this is the miasma of statistical data purporting to say something about the uneducated. The uneducated appear to be the illiterate; the illiterate, the high school dropouts. The data is less elitist than ludicrous. Hunter and Harman report that out of a total of 5,269,699 adults in South and North Carolina, 2,758,356 have dropped out of school— over 50 percent in both states (38). *The State* newspaper in South Carolina says that "nearly 400,000 South Carolinians 25 and older . . . never went to high school" ("Twenty Percent of Adults" C2). But the adult population of South Carolina in 1976 was 1,745,829. If Hunter and Harman's statistics are combined with *The State* newspaper's statistics, are we to believe that there are only 429,054 other nondropouts, nonilliterates left in the state? In 1989, *The State* reported that almost one out of three students quits high school in South Carolina ("State Board Declares"). This is related to the fact that "forty-two percent of adults do not graduate from high school, and nearly half of the students receive their school lunches for free or at a discount because they are disadvantaged." This same article reports that a bill in the legislature would attempt to cut the dropout rate by requiring students to be in school to obtain a driver's license. Given the precedent for illiteracy baiting, why not? The statistical yield would correlate illiterates with nondrivers, the uninsured, free-lunch eaters, and so on. The face of illiteracy is less and less linguistic.

The literacy/dropout equation is less vindictive, however, than other correlations. Deeply believed about illiteracy is its strong relationship with antisocial behavior. Even scholars who deny causal relationships between illiteracy and social trespass recount the dualities. Kozol, for example, notes that prison populations have the highest concentrations of adult illiterates in the country (13), and Hunter and Harman print table after table of the numbers of high school dropouts, people on welfare, people who fail to achieve an eighth-grade education, the weekly earnings of blacks and whites, and the wages of the hard-core unemployed. *Children in Need*, a document from the Committee for Economic Development in Washington, reports that "high school boys with poor grades are six times as likely as boys earning above-average grades to get in trouble with the law" (in *"At Risk Students"*). Welfare mothers and unwed teenage mothers constitute another cohort of suspected illiterates, a group especially noxious to taxpayers who believe to wipe them out is to ease an unfair tax burden ("Considerations for the Future").

Certainly, illiteracy is a fact of disfranchised life. It is not on a par with pregancy, however, or abuse, or criteria for imprisonment. That is, illiteracy is neither a trespass nor, actually, a redress. While almost nobody believes this, few are willing to shoulder the responsibilty for doing something about social exploitation in literacy programs. The content of literacy programs is evidence enough.

Most literacy programs model the first grade. The oldest and most widespread is the Laubach program. The founding slogan of the program is "Each One Teach One." The slogan assumes that advantaged people will help the disadvantaged. "That's what it's all about. Not only teach [illiterates] to read but also help them to help themselves up" (Gaik 6). The pedagogical process is grinding. Adult students work through series of workbooks, graduating from level to level until acceptable levels of reading and comprehension have been attained. Whereas the African Vai illiterate requires three or four days to become literate, and many American six- and seven-year-olds conquer literacy in a few months, Laubach assumes that the task takes years. A Laubach volunteer in a small town in the South praises the progress of a 35-year-old textile worker: "We're right on target. It's our 10th session and we're working on our 10th lesson" (Higgins 1). At the end of the Laubach program, the organization presents certificates of completion. Such programs are ubiquitous across the country.

Some literacy programs have attempted to promote a speedy process, but speediness is mostly expedient rhetoric. In 1983, the National Adult Literacy Project, sanctioned by then-president Ronald Reagan, concentrated on quick fixes. It sought to

> emphasize immediate and high-impact payoffs. Given the short periods of time, the relatively small resources, the salience of the problem [of illiteracy] and the timeliness of the issue, the NALP [National Adult Literacy Project] should focus on high visibility, high impact, short time-frame goals . . . outcomes and the factors and policies that affect these outcomes. (Gaik 23)

The framers of the National Adult Literacy Project narrowed the goals of the program accordingly: "Restrict the scope of the project . . . to programs . . . which have as their central goal the improvement of functional literacy for a productive work-force" (Gaik 23).

A program in the prison system of West Virginia also subscribes to the quick fix. It is called "No read, no release." Inmates who do not learn to read in prison programs forfeit parole until they buy themselves out of prison with a marketable reading level (Marcus). A major literacy campaign in 1988 encouraged literates to "read for ten minutes and then think about what it would be like not to be able to read" (Literacy Volunteers of America). These readers were then encouraged to become literacy volunteers.

All of these programs, the pedagogically slow and the expediently fast, presume limitations. Reaching people, for one thing, is a hardship. Gaik, Hunter and Harman, and Kozol describe the inability of literacy efforts to accommodate the basic realities of the lives of the illiterate. Programs are located outside of target communities, there is little or no childcare, the literacy volunteers tend to be older white females from socioeconomic strata far removed from illiterates. Volunteerism is itself a problem. Laubach and the Literacy Volunteers of America recruit teachers on a strictly voluntary basis. Yet to do so is to trivialize the need for the programs and to blame volunteers for inadequate preparation. A typical newspaper story, "Group Closer to Fighting Illiteracy," headlines the efforts of a literacy campaign ready to help but lacking in clientele: "We have the tutors; we need the students" (Sadler). Even if the students are available, expectations are hardly revolutionary. How much can housekeepers expect after they have completed literacy programs, literacy volunteers ask. "People are really not going to go from the fifth grade reading level to law school," says a coordinator of a "Get Ready" literacy program designed to train people to work on an assembly line for Mack Trucks (Lewis). Literacy, despite its magic, slows with the age of the literates and illiterates alike.

The contradictions in the current literacy situation in this country are remarkable. These statistics themselves seem to be out of control. What does it mean, for example, not to know who illiterates are, yet to hunt them? What does it mean to have statistical discrepancies in the tens of millions? Are there no consequences of literacy that mitigate against such inchoate data? What other organizations, businesses, community agencies operate on such bizarre information? If we cannot even count the illiterates, then it is clear that the people most affected by illiteracy are the people least able to change the situation. Does this mean that the literate most concerned with the nonliterate are also powerless?

This issue is one that goes round and round, as Jordan, Irmscher, and others have demonstrated. It's a crucial argument because it divvies up responsibilities. Andrew Sledd, in an angry article in *College English*, comments on the vitiation of this circle. Scholars, he says, admit gross inequities in school opportunities for minorities and the poor, but they aver to more research for answers. Sledd moots the question of whether adults inside schools are responsible for the failure of students or whether the society is responsible for the failure of the schools. "All of the above," he says (504). Yet the central mystery remains. Why are only some people dissatisfied, not with the failure of schools to standardize their clientele but with the standardization itself? Most people in schools believe that what is broke is mendable; if not, it's not broke. They busy themselves poking through complimentary copies of textbooks or, as Sledd has it, doing research on the classes they teach poorly or do not teach at all. The greater issue, however, is what, if anything, will bring the literacy profession to its senses.

Certainly, the agenda is power. At the end of his article, Sledd asks almost lamely for teachers to "teach students something of democracy, of sister- and brotherhood, and of legitimate and rational authority" because "it might help." More forcefully, he says we could stop being dupes (506). But, aside from alienating the members of his own English department as well as those who take exception to vaguely perverse ideas like sisterhood, Sledd is a voice without portfolio. In any case, his conclusion is an admission of powerlessness, the end of the literacy trail a dead end.

The best solution is to expand the landscape. Literacy efforts may not be part of the usual domain of "education," most certainly college education, but literacy as well as English is a part of the larger Western effort to educate the citizenry. That effort produces the most remarkably numerous generalizations about the success of education. The odd, but not inconsistent, situation here is that postsecondary education is held less accountable than other sorts. To wit, the greatest body of literature about the success and failure of education deals with kindergarten through twelfth grade. The terms of concern shift from, say, literacy to the dropout rate or to scores on standardized tests. The evidence, however, is unmistakable and directly aligned with the results obtained by postsecondary institutions. We have only to pinpoint several salient statistics.

Usually, such educational statistics fall under general observations of cataclysm. The 1986 Report of the National

Commission on the Role and Future of State Colleges and Universities titled *To Secure the Blessings of Liberty* provides an example:

> The storm warnings are unmistakable; our society is troubled; our economy is endangered; our democratic values jeopardized; our international leadership threatened; our educational system embattled. (3)

The report cites the contraction of the "educational pipeline" as the high school dropout rate exceeds 25 percent, "reaching levels as high as 45-50 percent for minorities in disadvantaged urban areas" (3). (Corollary to this last group, the report estimates that "up to 40 percent of minority adolescents have been found to be functionally illiterate" [3]).

A 1988 report, "Access to Knowledge: Breaking Down School Barriers to Learning," commissioned by the Education Commission of the States and supported by the College Board, recites a litany of chilling circumstances:

- The quality of education children receive can be predicted—to a considerable degree—by their race. Black, Hispanic, and other non-Asian minorities will not receive equal or high-quality opportunities in schools.
- The quality of education children receive can be predicted—to a considerable degree—by their parents' income. . . .
- The quality of education a child receives can be predicted— to a considerable degree—by his or her gender. . . .
- [S]tudents in schools with high rates of poverty share similar characteristics as students personally experiencing long-term poverty.
- Classifications [of students] according to ability often reflect language and cultural diversity rather than actual differences in capacity.
- Those who stand to benefit from classrooms with rich resources (motivated teachers, successful classmates, enriched curricula) always get the least. (Keating and Oakes 3–4)

These assertions are borne out by state and local statistics. In South Carolina, for example, in 1987 the annual dropout rate for the wealthiest district in the state was 1.2 percent or 46 out of 3,769 students; for the poorest district it was 6.8 percent, or 64 out of 948 students. For that same district, the percentage of students eligible for "free lunch" was 83.6 percent. In the wealthiest district, 4.0 percent of the families in 1979 were below the poverty level; in the poorest, 32.8 percent (*Rankings*). In 1986–1987 in South Carolina, about 47 percent of the children in public schools were nonwhite; in three years, that figure will exceed 50 percent. In 1986–1987, 22 percent of the teachers in the state were black; by the year 2000, that figure will decrease to 10 percent (WICHE).

And what of the college scene?

Without even bothering to notice how many students never reach college or looking at graduation statistics (which fail to interdict the precollege failure of the poor and minority), we can simply review the median scores on the SAT exam. In 1986, the scores were this: on the verbal part of the test, blacks scored 346, whites 449. Median scores according to race and income produced black verbal performance of 298 for those students whose family income was under $6,000; at the same income level, white students scored 415 on the verbal portion. Blacks in that income bracket constituted 12.9 percent of the total; whites, 1.8 percent. At the high end of income level ($50,000 or more), whites scored 60 points higher than blacks on the verbal test; 25.6 percent of the total whites made up that income category; 6.3 percent of the total blacks ("SAT Scores").

College enrollment of minorities, which has always reflected discrepancies in SAT scores, continues to drop. Since 1976, participation in college for low-income black students has dropped from 40 to 30 percent; and from 50 to 35 percent for Hispanic students. The decline in college participation for middle class black students from the early 1970s until 1988 has been 36 percent ("College Participation").

The only certainty is that to be poor and minority is to inherit dismal chances of reaching college, at least those that partly base admissions on SAT scores.

These figures are not really news to most educators. Attention to the data waxes and wanes as enrollment figures do the same. Rarely, however, do English educators step outside the circle of such educational embarrassment. The educational issues of such scores are tricky enough; adding to the tangle seems hardly productive or, perhaps more kindly put, out of one's field of expertise. The precise argument—indeed, the overall argument—is that the field of English expertise should be other than it is. Surely, we are affected by issues of access and testing whether we embrace the argument or not.

Expertise is no small matter, however, and it is forthright to ask how much of the world English is to make sense of and how. Another way to ask is how English teachers may meld the expertise of others with their own. The traditions of the English discipline have not merely mitigated against collaboration but may have overstated the difficulty. What, an English teacher might ask, am I to do about household incomes of less than $6,000? Put this way, the question is daunting. We remain content to simply allow equations between illiteracy and incivility, and to nod our heads at unfair but apparently unfathomable relationships between lack of English "skills" and lack of opportunity. One reason is the inutility of the question. A better question is, "Why is family income a concern only at the failing end of the educational continuum?" (English teachers might ask, more specifically, "Why is English the scapegoat when things go wrong?") The answers, though not simple, may be simpler than they appear.

For example, in testimony before the Human Resources Committee of the Commission on the Future of the South in 1986, Carol W. Williams, a specialist in public-health policy, reported a gross disparity in income. While the median income in 1983 for two-parent families was $27,329, for single-parent white families, the median was $12,239, and for single-parent black families, the median was $8,000 (5). Her testimony read:

> For children in female-headed families, the poverty rate was 54% [in 1984] as compared to 12.5% in other families. . . . When race is considered, 2 of every 3 black children and 1 of every 2 white children in single-parent families are poor. (5)

In the entire United States in 1986, the income of 3,112,000 households headed by women was under $10,000 (Hacker, 13).

Robert Hamrin describes the distribution of income in America. In 1986, "the top twenty percent of all American households received 46.1 percent of all pretax and pretransfer income." On the other hand, "the bottom twenty percent received 3.8 percent" (Hamrin). That is, 20 percent of the poorest Americans live on nearly nothing. Some other data further contextualize these figures. In 1988, 3.74 million families were dependent on welfare, double the number in 1970. Twenty percent of American children live in poverty

(Tisdall). We might keep in mind that in 1990, the U.S. budget was 1.2 trillion dollars.

What syntheses are we to draw among these figures, the dropout rate, and English departments? Before answering, let's look at one more piece of information, information on the contemporary work scene in the United States.

In an article in *The Nation* in 1989, William Serrin analyzes what has been called the "new work." He finds little new about it:

> Half the jobs created in the United States between 1979 and 1987 paid wages below the poverty level for a family of four. . . . What keeps families out of poverty is extra income. Just like the old days, everybody often has to work: mothers, fathers, and teenage children. (270)

We might consider this in light of the statistics just viewed of the numbers and poverty of single-parent households, households that clearly do not have extra workers—until, of course, children become old enough either to be put to work illegally or to drop out of school. We might also keep in mind that women, who occupy an increasing share of the job market, continue to be relegated to low-paying, traditional service jobs. Serrin concludes that "the New Work is largely a myth. . . . Most continue to do what the old workers have always done: a lot of scut work, often at relatively low pay, in many cases for the most demanding bosses" (272).

One type of scut work, and still mostly female work, is literacy work. Literacy scut work is better than other kinds for those lucky enough to be literate (though this is not a prima facie claim). The important realization is less an elaboration of the connections (as we did in the first chapter) than a close observation of how what we do intersects with what we do not do. Our statistics on working women and impoverished children are a case in point. College English teachers do not, for example, teach *as a matter of course* unemployed or impoverished minority women. They do not, *as a matter of course,* teach many or most of their children, even those who graduate from high school. The people they teach are the people who are not in the statistics just recited.

To be quite frank, at the precise point at which literacy becomes "functional," English teachers in the United States become dysfunctional. They, as well as the failed students, lose contact with literacy, and the teaching they continue to do becomes even more confined. This is because the population to which it is addressed is weeded out. By the ninth grade, the population of American schools is already an elite one.

This argument is as complex as it is undeniable. Many English teachers, probably most, do not feel that they teach elite populations. Yet these teachers appear to be suited to some students and not to others. Those to whom they are unsuited go away, at least eventually. Those to whom they are suited may not need them. This is the circle that ends in the unemployment and exploitation of poor women and children. It is the answer to the English teacher's question, "Why me?"

This issue has been addressed from widely different political perspectives. It is relatively easy to rehearse the political and educational platform of the right wing. Its basic tenet is that literacy civilizes the uncivilized. (Whether or not intended, the first argument for this comes from Goody and Watt's equation of literacy with a democratic society.) Any number of spokesmen (and most of the right speakers are white, tenured, middle-aged, middle class men) provide literate examples of what the right wants. Allan Bloom is hard to best:

> Actually openness results in American conformism—out there in the rest of the world is a drab diversity that teaches only that values are relative, whereas here [in education/college] we can create all the lifestyles we want. Our openness means we do not need others. Thus what is advertised as a great opening is a great closing. No longer is there hope that there are great wise men in other places and times who can reveal the truth about life—except for the few remaining young people who look for a quick fix from a guru. (34)

Bloom, of course, does not equate the truth of wise men with their literacy because, given the nature of his assumptions about wiseness, he does not have to.

E. D. Hirsch is less subtle. Those who would be literate need only consult the vocabulary list of civilization at the end of *Cultural Literacy*. They better do it quickly, also, as Hirsch predicts the doom of civilization already under way:

> To miss the opportunity of teaching young (and older) children the traditional materials of literate culture is a tragically wasteful mistake that deprives them of the information they would continue to find useful in later life. The inevitable effect of this fundamental educational mistake has been a

gradual disintegration of cultural memory, causing a gradual decline in our ability to communicate. The mistake has therefore been a chief cause of illiteracy, which is a subcategory of the inability to communicate. (113)

Hirsch is very generous in his recognition that literacy is a "subcategory" of communication, yet the relative socioeconomic positions of the communicants hardly requires another subcategorization.

Hirsch did not discover the meaning of cultural literacy on his own, nor is it a new concept. As Robert Rothman reports in *Education Week* in 1989, "The canon of required literature in public secondary schools differs little from what was in vogue 25 years ago, a study by a federally funded research center has found" (6). Shakespeare continues to lead the top ten "most assigned works," while *Huckleberry Finn* and *To Kill a Mockingbird* replace *Our Town*, *Silas Marner*, and *Great Expectations* in the top five. In fact, three Shakespeare plays make the top five in 1988 as opposed to only two in the top five in 1963 (6).

Worries of diminished standards for literacy also permeate the popular media and the local press. For example, one small-town Southern newspaper commented on the failure rate on a state-mandated high school exit exam. In 1986, barely 50 percent of all students in the state passed the trial exam. The failures were mostly poor black teenagers. The editorial in another small-town newspaper was dour: "One discouraging aspect of the test was the low score of many black students." The reason? "Experimental methods of education introduced in the last 15 or 20 years have failed the very children they were designed to help, and they have been cheated out of training in basics so essential to coping in this world" ("Low Exit Test Scores"). The tip-off is the reference to "basics." "Basics" is English (with a hat-tip to addition and subtraction). In 1990, the first year when the exit exam determined whether or not students could graduate, 3,057 students out of the 4,042 who failed the exam were black. The greatest obstacle was the writing portion of the exam. The state superintendent of schools called the results of the exam "encouraging," and said they were good for the work force in the state (Sponhour).

Perhaps the greatest curiosity in the conservative position is that although the right decries the slippage of the underclass, it is most worried about the flagrance with which middle class children treat English masters. What is going to happen to the world if its solid citizens rebuke the origins of solidity? Standardized tests may weed out the illiterate incompetents, but they also reflect an urgent impulse to regroup. The problem is that the most availed students do not want to go back to the haven of the elders. They want to go ahead, literacy be damned. The Johnny who can't write appreciates writing only to the extent that it promises a salary high enough to employ a secretary. The truth of the matter, of course, is that this is a legitimate position, legitimate because it achieves the same aims as conservative literacy.

If the conservative position can be characterized as introverted, the liberal—and the left—position is extroverted. The right is interested to maintain a type of person; the left, to promote many types. On that score, too, one might observe that the right tends to appear unified and solid; the left, on the other hand, seems made up of individuals, an irony probably lost less on the right than on the left.

Nonetheless, proponents of liberal education, liberal literacy, unite on one issue. This is the value and necessity of community. If communities—particularly disfranchised communities—*are* valued, then, the thinking goes, the mechanisms that disbar them not only lose their force but dominated people begin to realize ways to assert their rights. The idealistic extension of this idea is that a society whose energies have been spent on maintaining inequality can also come to realize the benefits of parity.

Perhaps the most eloquent American spokesperson for this position is Michael Holzman. In "The Social Context of Literacy Education," he writes:

> If we are to help people remain in school, if we are to educate those who do, if we are to encourage those who return to some form of schooling after dropping out, we must match the resistance to schooling. Just as every manifestation of the system of domination is in a sense a replication of the entire system, so every human interaction, insofar as it is human, presents the possibility of human freedom. The point is to make human interactions possible by forming socially beneficial equivalents of gangs, neighborhoods, and street-corner associations that will enable those who are not encouraged by their cultural environment to value schooling to do so. *Only in school are people who fail to decode a text not helped by those around them.* [emphasis added] ("This is a test" 137)

Whereas Holzman may have underestimated the rife competitiveness—or the tragic childhood violence—that penetrates homes (middle class homes, broken homes, extended homes), he nails the idea of education to the practice of education. In all of the liberal propositions to improve literacy, one feature recurs: equate literacy with equality and literacy will take care of itself.

Liberal educators, in fact, have been saying this for years. Daniel Fader in the late 1960s created a program called Hooked-on-Books in a juvenile prison. He made available paperback books in quantity to juvenile offenders. The kids read the books. Peter Medway and Mike Torbe, teaching working-class British high school students in the mid-1970s, created a program of student writing and reasoning that went way beyond the usual expectations for working-class students. James Moffett, an American educator, proposed also in the 1970s a "model of public schooling based on the incorporation of school sites and educators into a community-wide network for sharing all locally available human and material resources." And Jonathan Kozol proposed a grassroots effort composed of "circles of learners" within neighborhood centers.

Perhaps the idea with the greatest scope (and publicity) was proposed by Hunter and Harman. Their original Ford Foundation study came out in 1979, to which was added a long preface in a 1985 reissue. Hunter and Harman recommended a community-based response to illiteracy in America, a response that would link community literacy work with other programs to eliminate social inequities:

> ... [W]e support programs that increase the skills of community members to interact with and change the mainstream culture and its institutions. This would incorporate the positive values of the communities and enable their members to participate more fully in the social and economic life of the broader society. (105)

Too, Hunter and Harman recognize that literacy means money; a good literacy program includes "counseling, transportation, child-care, one-to-one recruitment, in-home service, non-print information, and electronic media delivery services . . . "(100). In other words, literacy programs must correspond to social needs. Likewise, the theory of language must correspond to a contextual agenda. Labov said this earlier than most. In his 1960s study of black male youths in northern ghettos, he said that language learning must go on according to knowledge, not rote learning. If a city teacher, for example, is to deal with a ghetto child, "it means that the social situation is the most powerful determinant of verbal behavior and that an adult must enter into the right social relationship with a child if he wants to find out what a child can do." Labov concludes, "This is just what many teachers cannot do" (212).

Torbe and Medway assert similar theories of language. Of working-class students they reiterate:

> [W]e cannot kit them out with a complete new language and style of behavior as they come in through the classroom door. Our interest as teachers is in further learning, not producing speakers who are more respectably turned out. The language for learning *must* be in the first place the speakers' own familiar language; after all, we are asking it to perform the function of thinking, and it will need to come as easily and naturally as thought; that is why it needs to be the language which the students wear as close to them as their skins. (42)

When William Bennett in the early 1980s was the United States Secretary of Education, he wrote a booklet of teaching tips to improve the education of American youth. Among the suggestions for running a tight ship, he recommended that children be taught to read by the phonics method. Sight reading, he claimed, is largely responsible for childhood illiteracy. Abandon sight reading, gain literacy, problem solved (Connell). Though Terrell Bell before him was hardly so simplistic, *A Nation at Risk* presumes that if American students were just taught to comprehend and write decently, they would beat their adversaries. (Bell, like many who come after him, is also concerned with scientific and mathematical literacy.) Nearly everyone agrees that literacy is an important feature of American life. Which American life is the only quibble.

The right is relatively untroubled by American life; the right knows a proper lifestyle and wishes to maintain it. The left is caught between the knowledge of what constitutes comfort and the knowledge that much Western comfort comes at the expense of the poor and minorities. The result of this is a left that sometimes sounds like the right, and a right that can say and do anything that strikes its fancy.

What to do? What to do?

The sorrow of the left is its inability to examine—if not rid itself of—a deeply embedded trust in middle class values.

Marilyn Cooper, writing powerfully for the need of English teachers to examine their values, still locates the solution to literacy problems in gentle benevolence. Of English teachers as a group she writes:

> We believe in the value of critical thinking, cognitive disso-nance, and adopting different perspectives—all of which are based on the central value of coming to know through reading and writing. But that these are the norms of our discourse community, that they are *our* values, is not itself a sufficient reason for us to offer them to students so persuasively. *Why* are these things valuable to us and to our students? This is the question that is not addressed in the discussions of collabora-tive learning and discourse communities; it is the question we must answer if we are to persuade students to adopt our community as their own. (55)

The last "if" shoots the argument in the foot. The conclu-sion retains the view of the safe, benevolent inside, the place where we are and a place others might be persuaded to inhabit. Whereas Cooper, in all probability, speaks less of class values than realistic economics, unless teachers always teach those from the groups out of which the teachers emerge, we will not get very far trying to create new opportunities based on a wel-come mat. The reality is that middle class safety is less an opportunity than a staging ground.

Another version of this conundrum is described by Anthony Petrosky. Petrosky is a literacy researcher. He is hired by a pres-tigious college and a rich foundation. He researches the poorest county in Mississippi. The county sends most of its students to postsecondary education. Unlike most students in the same socioeconomic categories, these students pass standardized tests. Petrosky has spent a good amount of time assessing why. At the Modern Language Association's Right to Literacy Con-ference in Columbus, Ohio, in September 1988, he described the English courses at the high school in the county. The courses proceed like this:

TEACHER: What kind of books are on the back wall?
STUDENTS: Periodicals.

TEACHER: Dictionary. You all know what a dictionary is, right?
CLASS: (in unison) Yes.

TEACHER: Give me five things we use a dictionary for.
CLASS: (silence)
TEACHER: Write that down. Look it up for tomorrow.

TEACHER: What does a predicate adjective do?
CLASS (in unison): Completes the linking verb and describes the subject.
TEACHER: The cake tastes delicious. Delicious is what part of speech?

Petrosky says that this pedagogy goes on every day in the classrooms of the poorest county in Mississippi. He says that the students who pass the tests and go on to postsecondary education do not come back to the county. The county has no jobs. The students do not become teachers.

What did Petrosky think of the educational situation in the poorest county in Mississippi? He was ambivalent. He refused to advocate the pedagogy; he refused to decry it. He had to shrug his shoulders when asked if other poor counties should adopt the pedagogy.

In the states of the Union with any sizable poor or minority population, the remedial classes are jammed with the poor and the minority; entire schools in the urban areas of the North constitute remedial pens. In 1984, Texas administered competency tests to graduates of the state's schools of education: 84 percent of the black graduates failed reading; 80 percent of the black graduates failed writing (Hechinger). Researchers predict that if current trends continue, 96 percent of all black candidates to teach will be denied entry into the teaching profession. By 1990, these researchers predict that only 5 percent of the teachers in the United States will be black (Hechinger). The overwhelming nature of these failures suggests a monolith of insurmountable problems and pedagogies.

In *Horace's Compromise*, Theodore Sizer writes of two facts about high schools that strike him forcefully. The first is uniformity:

> As one visits communities one is gradually struck by how similar the structure and articulated purpose of American high schools are. Rural schools, city schools; rich schools, poor schools; public schools, private schools; big schools, little schools; the *framework* of grades, schedules, calendar, courses of studies, even rituals is astonishingly uniform and has been so for at least forty years. . . . High school is a kind of

> secular church, a place of national rituals that mark the
> stages of a young citizen's life. The value of its rites appears
> to depend on national consistency. (5–6)

Yet Sizer's second observation is entirely inconsistent with his
first.

> Among schools there was one important difference, which
> followed from a single variable only: the social class of the
> student body. . . . It got so that I could say with some justifica-
> tion to school principals, "Tell me about the incomes of your
> students' families and I'll describe your school." (6)

The point is not that poor schools do not run along similar
lines as wealthy schools—a broken school bell still implies
investment in noisy rituals—but that enormous differences
exist inside appearances of similarity.

The differences *are* enormous. In South Carolina, for example, there are 91 school districts. The median size of the districts is 3,748 students but some districts have fewer than
600 students while the largest district has more than 50,000.
School boards in those districts also vary in size and in the way
they are constituted. Some school boards are popularly elected;
others are appointed by legislators; and others are appointed by
other boards (Norton and Rex 4). According to a recent "Education Background Paper" written for the South Carolina
Assembly on the Future:

> The governing board of the S. C. School Boards Association
> takes the position that all school boards . . . should have the
> authority to "raise, at a minimum, the local funds needed to
> comply with the state and federal requirements." (Norton and
> Rex 5)

Yet what ability, one might ask, does a school district of 600
students have to raise sums to meet the requirements applied
to districts significantly bigger and richer?

Within schools across the country, there is also substantial
variation in the amount of time students spend in educational
activity. Reginald M. Clark reports to the Academy for Educational Development that American students spend between
"7.5 to 17.5 hours of cogitation per week" or "270–430 hours
per year in the process of learning in the typical school classroom" (8). Some schools, however, exceed this rate, providing

"an additional 160 hours per year" of education in "essential skills." Clark observes, "At this rate, by the end of the fifth grade, high-achieving youngsters will have engaged in the learning process at school as much as or more than low-achieving ninth-graders" (8).

The same differences apply to school materials and student/teacher ratios. According to *The Harvard Education Letter*, a reading textbook for first-graders contains 716 "new words," while another contains only 388. By the end of the first grade, students in districts with high proportions of black children "could read significantly fewer words than children of comparable ability who had more hours of instruction" ("First Grade" 5). In 1987, in Washington, DC, the student-teacher ratio was roughly 14:1; in California, it was 23:1.

The barometers of success are unnerving. The newspaper that goes to every South Carolina public school exclaimed in 1989:

> For the first time in 20 years, South Carolina no longer trails the nation in Scholastic Aptitude Test scores. Neighboring state North Carolina now holds the bottom ranking with scores averaging 836 on the SAT, a drop of five points from the previous year. (Harper 1)

Such is the educational establishment in America. It hardly seems to be a smoothly working system. How did American education get to be this way? The question is not rhetorical. Do we look for one cause or a number of causes? Do we interrogate a federal or state agency, a school system, a board of education, a student body, a legislature, a school of education, academic writers of commissioned reports, a tradition of educational measurement, the enfranchised or the disfranchised? Do we, in fact, engage the mess, thereby becoming part of it?

In order to entertain this question, we must understand what we have already done. This is difficult to do, not because we have done little but because we have rarely accounted for what we do. Certainly, every generation has decried the literacy of those who have come after it, and blasted those responsible for the deterioration; but denunciation in the United States took a particularly frantic tone in the late 1970s when books like *The Literacy Hoax* and the variety of news coverage of Johnny's inability to both read and write reached the front pages. The inability indicated more than ineptitude. Claimed the author of *The Literacy Hoax:* unlike the less than 20 percent of American college students who take American Literature, "the average Soviet high-school student is assigned a minimum of thirty books a year in his literature courses, and reports indicate that the average number of books read is closer to one hundred per year" (Copperman 99). The most important thing for the English profession to understand is that while it stood by during the catastrophe, it was also used.

We have seen how literacy engages socioeconomics in a literate economy. We have seen that access to a literate economy is through education. We have seen that the arbiter of education is the test. We have seen that the test reduces to poverty or maintains in it entire segments of the economy. What we have to see, also, is how literacy is a weapon, the knife that severs the society and slices the opportunities and rights of its poorest people.

This is true on the most trivial level. From the California Test of Basic Skills to the Scholastic Aptitude Test, question after question demands decisions on grammar, usage, comprehension, referencing, and so on. Some standardized tests possess writing components. Scores on writing samples, often determined by "'socialized readers,'" are averaged into the "objective" scores, and the sum constitutes the pass rate. The great bulk of such tests consists of multiple-choice questions; and standardized tests made of multiple-choice questions constitute literate occasions of social entrapment.

Arguably, most questions are vacuous, discrete, and random. A typical question on an entry test into the teaching profession asks prospective candidates if "a roomful of breathless people" means no one in the room is breathing. Porter Sexton in an article for the College Board magazine analyzes a long, involved question surveyed by the National Assessment of Education Progress to determine if students were passably literate. The question was about bus schedules. Sexton's summary of the question is apt:

> The real problem with this question is not that it has so many "right" answers ... but that it is insulting. It insults the individual asked to answer the question by displaying an unreasonable facsimile of a bus schedule. Readers aren't at the corner [catching a bus]; they are sitting somewhere with this test. One is tempted to respond: "If I can't catch a bus, how the hell do you think I got here?" This is clearly a put-up job. Its purpose is to try to separate readers from their understanding. It doesn't ask readers, "Would you use this fake

schedule and if so how?" Rather, it dictates to readers what they should consider. Instead of promoting or even allowing, creative thought (or *any* thought), it stifles it in favor of mindlessly following directions and selecting a "correct" answer. It is implicitly judgmental and it is precisely the type of insult that is now so popularly being hurled at our nation's youth. (4)

The insult is deeper than a brush stroke across American youth, however. Few architects of standardized tests, for example, would use the schedule of the Concorde, since the literacy required to read the Concorde schedule hardly meets the criteria for competence, not to mention the regulations of multiple choice. The Concorde flies too limited a schedule.

The insult is the pervasive lie that language makes the difference, a lie that goes to the heart not merely of English in the institution but of the public perception of English. To speak of standardized tests as literacy tests is itself a subterfuge, for the literacy tested is hardly plural. Standardized literacy tests are tests of standard English, and standard English is held to be the benchmark of opportunity. This belief is so ingrained that even those who would presume to be on opposite sides of the fence agree that the foundation of the fence is solid. William Raspberry, a black, liberal editorialist, and Michael Skube, a white, Southern book editor—both of whose columns are syndicated—provide a startling example.

"Standard English Should Be Required" and "Black English Imprisons Blacks" sound like story headlines written by the same hand. In this case, Raspberry wrote the first, Skube the second. Skube begins his article,

> Fifteen years ago, before the hangover had set in, the Conference on College Composition and Communication stood to deliver these woozy words before stumbling home: "Once a teacher understands the arbitrary nature of the oral and written forms, the pronunciation or spelling of a word becomes less important than whether it communicates what the student wants to say." The lights were not yet out on the aggressively egalitarian spirit of public education that began in the 1960s, but this was just about the last call. (3D)

Skube is not amused. "Standard English—It is our language, remember?" he asks. Of course, Raspberry is not amused either:

> The sort of English, written and spoken, that we automatically associate with intelligence. . . . Standard English—not

Cajun or hillbilly or West Indian patois or Black English—is the language that marks an American man or woman as educated." (12A)

Raspberry and Skube agree on other points. Black English is fine, within limits.

Raspberry:

> A sympathetic but tough teacher might tell her young charges that it is of no concern to her what language they use on the playground. But in her classroom, the only acceptable dialect is standard English. . . . If everybody had to speak the standard in the classroom, the stigma [of standard English to blacks] would disappear. (12A)

Skube:

> I, too, once taught in a black elementary school. It was a rural school in Louisiana in the late 1960s, a parish and people wonderfully evoked in the novels of Ernest J. Gaines. . . . For two years, I heard black English all around me, from the principal and other teachers as much as from the students, and came to have, I think, a good appreciative ear for its rhythms and inflections. I also came to think of it as a prison. Students who were otherwise intelligent could not express themselves intelligently except to one another, and had still greater trouble expressing themselves on paper. (3D)

The playground is not the chief concern of either Raspberry or Skube, of course.

Skube:

> From my own experience I knew that [black English] was a language that was rich and vivid and evocative and many other good things, but one that would only lead most of my students back to the quarters and the cane fields. If they wanted to become writers, they would become dialect writers—not a bad thing, but a limiting thing; if they wanted to become teachers, they would likely have to pursue their ambitions through the historically black colleges; if they wanted to become engineers or scientists—well they could forget about that. (3D)

Raspberry:

> I see nothing but good coming from helping young people— black youngsters in particular—acquire facility with the only language that confers instant respect. (12A)

Skube agrees:

> I don't know about black English, but I know about the other
> [standard English]. It is not enough merely to be understood.
> It matters what you write, but it matters also how you write
> it. It is a reflection of your mind, and a mind, as the United
> Negro College Fund knows, is a terrible thing to waste. And,
> even worse, to imprison. (3D)

In 1865, the National Educational Association—the
NEA—held its annual convention. The incoming president of
the association was a high school principal from Harrisburg,
Pennsylvania. The *History of the American Teachers Association*, the black American teachers' association, summarizes
the president-elect's address:

> He reviewed the Civil War, denounced slavery and ex-slave
> holders, and declared that no seceded state should be admit-
> ted to the Union until it provided constitutionally for a free
> school system. He declared that Negroes should be prepared
> by teachers for all citizenship rights and that teachers should
> instruct both black people and poor whites so that there
> should be no re-establishment of slavery. (Perry 29)

The president-elect said nothing about literacy. Even then, he,
like Allan Bloom today, did not have to.

The *History* chronicles the path of free schooling. At the
turn of the century:

> The Southern states, where most Blacks lived, were uniform
> in prohibiting black and white children from attending
> school together. Typical was the Florida statute of 1895
> which made it a penal offense for any group within the state
> to conduct a school of any grade—public, private, or paro-
> chial—in which white persons and Negroes should be
> boarded together, instructed in the same room or by the same
> teacher. (34)

What reason did the *History* give? The reason was economic:

> That law and others of similar intent reinforced what was
> generally known, namely, that black education, freely admin-
> istered, might inspire the recipients to demand racial equal-
> ity.... Other contributing factors were the dearth of money
> in the Southern states to support any system of education,
> much less two systems; the fear that education would spoil
> Negroes for labor; the fear that literacy would qualify Blacks

for voting, and the conviction that whites (as the superior people) should be served first, with the "colored" getting whatever small amount might be left for education. (34)

These observations from one hundred and twenty years ago are still applicable to the educational system in this country, despite the extent to which the system tries to disguise itself as egalitarian. Twenty-five years ago the black educational system that had been laboriously established, despite all of the under-funding and restrictions in the South, was dismantled under the guise of equal access. Integration may have been a laudable goal, just as teaching literacy to the illiterate is. But the society that wrought the educational change just as quickly ensured that those newly integrated into it would find themselves dom-inated by white middle class teachers and administrators who would institute or reinforce policy to ensure the maintenance of white middle class values and opportunities at the expense of others and who would use literacy to do it.

June Jordan at the National Council of Teachers of English conference asks, *What to do? What to do?* To answer that ques-tion, we must understand the connections between literacy and economy, literacy and work, literacy and race, gender and class, literacy and English teachers. We must understand the extraordinary power of the educational process and of literacy standards not merely to exclude citizens from participating in the country's economic and political life but to brand them and their children with indelible prejudice, the prejudice of lan-guage. We must reform the educational process to demand diversity, to destroy, as Johnnetta Cole says, the myth that "excellence is impossible if there is diversity." We must, more-over, revise our notions of "standardization" and "excellence," junking most of them and not feeling compelled to replace what was wrong. We must take responsibility for the racism throughout schooling, the racism leveled most brutally and effectively in children's earliest years of schooling by literacy whose achievements can be seen in the loss of a third or more poor students by schooling's end. We must stop being almost hysterically convinced that students who cannot read or write the standard language cannot "make it." Students of nonstan-dard languages in the United States do not fail because of a language failure; they fail because they live in a society that lies about language. We in English in an information economy in a country that calls itself free make the lie palpable.

In the late 1940s, Septima Poinsette Clark set up citizenship schools all across the South. The schools existed in the back rooms of boarded-up stores and in the basements of churches—anywhere that white people did not go or would not suspect. The students attended at night. In those schools, in two or three months, Clark taught illiterate black laborers to read the Constitution of the United States. She taught them to read the Constitution so that they could vote. She says,

> People thought I had new-fangled ideas.... But my new-fangled ideas worked out. I didn't know they were going to work out though. I just thought that you couldn't get people to register and vote until you teach them to read and write. That's what I thought and I was so right. (Brown 53)

Just before Clark died in her late eighties, she said,

> Education is my big priority now. I want people to see children as human beings and not to think of the money that it costs nor to think of the time it will take, but to think of the lives that can be developed into Americans who will redeem the soul of America and will really make America a great country. This is my feeling now. (Brown 121)

Notice the last line in the following document reprinted in a popular American magazine in 1988. The document is a pamphlet titled "Kitchen Spanish." It translated from English to Spanish the following:

> Do you have references?
> Do you know how to take care of children?
> This is your room.
> Dust here.
> Please be careful with this, it is breakable.
> Do not put this in the dryer.
> Please do not answer the phone.
> Wash this by hand.
> Do not use (Comet/steel wool), it will scratch the surface.
> Do not be afraid, it will not hurt you.

Do not be afraid, it will not hurt you. Certainly nothing less disingenuous about translation, about literacy, and about the subterfuge of language can be said. The truth is that literacy and English instruction can hurt you, more clearly and forcefully and permanently than it can help you, and that schools, like other social institutions, are designed to replicate, or at least not to disturb, social division and class privilege. In an information economy, schools require an emphasis on literacy, and literacy is the province of English teachers.

Some English teachers understand that English is a fraction of the real problem. Many of these English teachers are very angry; many are alone. Some find themselves in almost magical circumstances when money and help for special programs become available. These English teachers save many students. But they do not save enough. And when the special money that funds the special programs runs out, the savings account is closed.

In the beginning of *Negative Dialectics*, Theodor Adorno writes, "Philosophy, which once seemed obsolete, lives on because the moment to realize it was missed" (3). He means that some historical mistakes destroy other historical possibilities. He continues, "Theory cannot prolong the moment its critique depended on. A practice infinitely delayed is no longer the forum for appeals against self-satisfied speculation; it is mostly the pretext used by executive authorities to choke, as vain, whatever critical thoughts the practical change would require" (3). These things can be said, today, about literacy.

If literacy had always been fair, if literacy were a kaleidoscope, if literacy really made us human, then we might be sorry. But literacy was never this way, and it was wrong to think it was. We may not be better off to have missed it but we can at least be enlightened by its passing.

We are, nevertheless, still at an impasse. What to do with our profession, what to do with our mechanisms of oppression, what to do with our hysteria or complacency or resignation, what to do with the great disparities among our resources and knowledge and access to help, what to do with a world whose literacy pampers us but targets those we teach, what to do with a violent history, a miserly present, and a myopic future? What to do—we English teachers—to deal with all of that?

We either recognize that we already "deal with all of that" and continue to do it, or we recognize the unfairness of our dealings and stop. We promote greater literacy, or we promote greater humanity. The first choice is easy. The second choice is not. The second choice is infinitely more human, however. Perhaps one of the consequences of humanity is literacy. Perhaps one of the consequences of literacy is its failure to end the violence of an unfair society. Perhaps the consequences of both are to return the responsibility for violence to its rightful owners. That is who we are. Our only question is *What to do?*

CONCLUSION

It is probably true that literacy instructors and policy makers who accomplish the most hardbitten gains are rarely heard from. The same is probably also true for those who do the most damage. The paradox is infuriating because it appears impervious.

The fragmentation of school days and schedules and procedures exists because it achieves the same results as a well-run system, perhaps achieves them better. A single person in a single district or a single school or a single department can assume enormous burdens to effect change. She can spend her time, her money, her energy, her investment in belief. As long as she can go on, she is not stopped. Indeed, what finally stops her is herself. When she stops, more than herself is stopped. Once the reservoir is used up, it is gone.

This book claims that literacy is a blind alley. Must it claim, therefore, that everyone in the alley is either blind or is leading the blind?

Part of the answer lies in the inutility of the metaphor. The blind are merely sightless, not thoughtless. Everyone of us knows committed, extraordinary teachers, writers, and researchers. Many of the people noted in this book do brilliant, unprecedented work. Indeed, what is to explain this book if not the power of precedent?

Yet the paradox is shameless. To tell a State Department of Education (or an English department in a university, for that matter) that small, minority, poor children have beautiful language already, that impoverished teenage mothers are future doctors and teachers, that students write unnerving essays regardless of spelling is like telling the State it has jurisdiction. The State absorbs even what it rejects.

The truth is that many, many people tell superintendents, and departments of education, and English departments every day that current practice is not working, that new practice is possible, that evidence abounds for success in altered conditions, and that real change is less expensive than injustice. No matter how awful things get, some people keep hacking away.

What those many committed and aware people say matters a great deal. However, as long as they believe that arguments couched in literacy will change the circumstances of our work and the possibilities for a fair economy, then their work and ours will proceed piecemeal and will be welcomed and accepted. We can be right every day of the week, week after week.

This is not pessimism. It is system.

A system takes a lot of trouble. A system must be devised and implemented. To be sure, much of its design is tacit, its implementation an extension of usual modes of comfortable life. That is why most people who are uncomfortable in a system experience frustration. That is also why uncomfortable people can often change a system. They can see it.

For example, standardized (literacy) tests are not natural disasters. They are a system. One of the most powerful standardized tests came about when minority teachers won the legal right to receive equal pay with white teachers. Today, in some states, students take three different standardized tests each year. The number of educational officials required to tally the results of these tests triples. The appropriation of money a state spends on the tally is increased. The accreditation of officials and institutions to elaborate the results engenders additional supervision. This is how a system works.

It may be that the most likely way change will ever happen is incremental, local, one person at a time, one dedicated teacher, one brilliant researcher, one promising student. If so, perhaps despair over a system is a harbinger of its own death.

But this is a way of change, not a reason. Local change is not antithetical to the possibility of sweeping, fast, clear change. Too often, people perceive broad change only in terms of violence. They overlook the incremental, daily violence against those who are not favored by the system. Changing the way we teach, changing the literacy equation in schools and lives, does not require violence. It requires necessity.

Those who understand necessity understand literacy. Those who understand literacy are those to whom we must listen. Those to whom we must listen must ultimately become ourselves. In this way, the change that many of us want may become the change that all of us require.

REFERENCES

ADLER, MORTIMER J., et al. *The Paideia Proposal: An Educational Manifesto.* New York: Macmillan, 1982.

ADORNO, THEODOR W. *Negative Dialectics.* Trans. E. B. Ashton. New York: A Continuum Book, The Seabury Press, 1966.

All Things Considered. National Public Radio. KCRW, Santa Monica. 12 April 1985.

ARONOWITZ, STANLEY. *The Crisis in Historical Materialism: Class, Politics and Culture in Marxist Theory.* New York: Praeger, J. F. Bergin, Publishers, 1981.

———. *False Promises: The Shaping of American Working Class Consciousness.* New York: McGraw-Hill, 1973.

———. "Toward Redefining Literacy." *Social Policy.* 12.2 (1981): 53–55.

ARONOWITZ, STANLEY, and HENRY A. GIROUX. *Education Under Siege: The Conservative and Radical Debate Over Schooling.* Granby, MA: Bergin and Garvey, 1985.

BAILEY, RICHARD W., and ROBIN MELANIE FOSHEIM, eds. *Literacy for Life: The Demand for Reading and Writing.* New York: The Modern Language Association of America, 1983.

BATESON, GREGORY. *Steps to an Ecology of Mind.* New York: Ballantine Books, 1982.

BEACH, RICHARD, and DAVID PEARSON, eds. *Perspectives on Literacy: Proceedings of the 1977 Perspectives on Literacy Conference.*

Minneapolis/St. Paul: College of Education, University of Minnesota, 1978.

BELL, DANIEL. *The Coming of Post-Industrial Society: A Venture in Social Forecasting.* New York: Basic Books, 1973.

BLOOM, ALLAN. *The Closing of the American Mind.* New York: Simon and Schuster, 1987.

BLOUGH, DORIS. "Smaller Classes Benefit Students." Voice of the People. *Rock Hill Herald.* 25 February 1986: A4.

BORMUTH, JOHN. "Reply to Jack Merwin." Beach 64–71.

BOURDIEU, PIERRE, and JEAN-CLAUDE PASSERON. *Reproduction in Education, Society and Culture.* London: Sage Publications, 1977.

BRANDT, DEBORAH. "Versions of Literacy." *College English.* 47 (1985): 128–137.

BRITTON, JAMES, et al. *The Development of Writing Abilities (11–18).* London: Schools Council Publications, 1975.

BRITTON, JAMES. *Prospect and Retrospect: Selected Essays.* Ed. Gordon M. Pradl. Portsmouth, NH: Boynton/Cook, 1982.

BRAUDEL, FERNAND. *Capitalism and Material Life 1400–1800.* Trans. Miriam Kochan. New York: Harper Colophon Books, 1975; Libraire Armand Colin, 1967.

BROWN, CYNTHIA STOKES, ed. *Ready from Within: Septima Clark and the Civil Rights Movement.* Navarro, CA: Wild Trees Press, 1986.

BURKE, KENNETH. *Language as Symbolic Action: Essays on Life, Literature, and Method.* Berkeley, CA: University of California Press, 1966.

CAMPBELL, JEREMY. *Grammatical Man: Information, Entropy, Language and Life.* New York: Simon and Schuster, 1982.

Children in Need: Investment Strategies for the Educationally Disadvantaged. A Statement by the Research and Policy Committee. Washington, D. C.: The Committee for Economic Development, 1987. Commission on the Future of the South. Southern Growth Policies Board, 1986.

CHOMSKY, NOAM. *Aspects of a Theory of Syntax.* Cambridge: MIT Press, 1965.

CLARK, HERBERT, and EVE V. CLARK. *Psychology and Language: An Introduction to Psycholinguistics.* New York: Harcourt Brace Jovanovich, 1977.

CLARK, REGINALD M. "Critical Factors in Why Disadvantaged Students Succeed or Fail in School." Washington, D. C.: The Academy for Educational Development (1988), 1–19.

COLE, JOHNNETTA. "The Road to Higher Education: Realizing the Dream." *Higher Education and National Affairs.* 15 January 1990, 5.

"College Participation Rates Decline For Low-Income Minorities, ACE Finds." *Higher Education and National Affairs.* 39 (15 January 1990), 1–4.

CONNELL, CHRISTOPHER. " 'The Ram' Is Going the Distance—U. S. Secretary of Education William Bennett." Editorial/Impact. *The State* (Columbia, SC). 7 April 1986: B1.

COOPER, MARILYN. "Unhappy Consciousness in First-Year English: How to Figure Things Out for Yourself." Cooper and Holzman, 28–60.

COOPER, MARILYN, and MICHAEL HOLZMAN. *Writing as Social Action.* Portsmouth, NH: Boynton/Cook Heinemann, 1989.

COPPERMAN, PAUL. *The Literacy Hoax.* New York: Morrow, 1980.

CURTISS, SUSAN. *Genie: A Psycholinguistic Study of a Modern Day Wild Child.* New York: Academic Press, 1977.

D'ANGELO, FRANK. *A Conceptual Theory of Rhetoric.* Boston: Winthrop, 1975.

———. "Luria on Literacy: The Cognitive Consequences of Reading and Writing." Raymond 154–169.

DELATTRE, EDWIN J. "The Insiders." Bailey and Fosheim 52–59.

DENNISON, GEORGE. *The Lives of Children: A Practical Description of Freedom in Its Relation to Growth and Learning. The Story of the First Street School.* New York: Vintage Books, 1969.

DEWEY, JOHN. *Individualism, Old and New.* New York: Capricorn Books, 1972; G. P. Putnam's Sons, 1929.

DUCKWORTH, ELEANOR. "The Year of the Reports: Responses from the Educational Community." *Harvard Education Review.* 54 (1984): 15–20.

EAGLETON, TERRY. *Criticism and Ideology: A Study in Marxist Literary Theory.* London: Verso Editions, 1984.

ELBOW, PETER. *Writing with Power: Techniques for Mastering the Writing Process.* New York: Oxford UP, 1981.

FADER, DANIEL N., and ELTON B. MCNEIL. *Hooked on Books: Program and Proof.* New York: Putnam, 1968.

FANKEL, MARTIN M., ed. *Projections of Education Statistics to 1986–87.* National Center for Educational Statistics. U. S. Department of Health, Education and Welfare. Washington, D. C.: GPO, 1978.

FANON, FRANZ. *The Wretched of the Earth.* Trans. Constance Farrington. New York: Grove Press, Evergreen Black Cat Edition, 1968.

FINLAY, LINDA S., and VALERIE FAITH. "Illiteracy and Alienation in American Colleges: Is Paulo Freire's Pedagogy Relevant?" *Radical Teacher* 16 (1979): 28–37.

"First Grade Reading: Who Learns and Who Doesn't." *The Harvard Education Letter.* 3 (January 1987): 4–6.

FISH, STANLEY. *Is There a Text in This Class: The Authority of Interpretive Communities.* Cambridge: Harvard UP, 1980.

FLOWER, LINDA, and JOHN R. HAYES. "A Cognitive Process Theory of Writing." *College Composition and Communication* 32 (1981): 365–387.

FOUCAULT, MICHEL. *The Archaeology of Knowledge.* Trans. A. M. Sheridan Smith. London: Tavistock Publications, 1972.

FREIRE, PAULO. *Education for Critical Consciousness.* Trans. Myra Ramos. New York: Continuum, 1973.

———. "The Importance of the Act of Reading." *Journal of Education* 165 (1983): 5–11.

———. *Pedagogy of the Oppressed.* Trans. Myra Berman Ramos. New York: Continuum, 1981.

———. *The Politics of Education: Culture, Power and Liberation.* Trans. Donaldo Macedo. Granby, MA: Bergin and Garvey Publishers, Inc., 1985.

GAIK, FRANK. "Examining American Literacy Projects." Workplace Literacy in the Inner City. CCC Conference. Minneapolis, 21 March 1985.

GEERTZ, CLIFFORD. *Local Knowledge: Further Essays in Interpretive Anthropology.* New York: Basic Books, 1983.

GEPHARDT, RICHARD C. "Process and Intention: A Bridge from Theory to Classroom." *The Writing Instructor* 1 (1982): 135–145.

GIFFORD, RICHARD. "Communication Skills Improvement Program." Making or Breaking the Marginal Reader. NCTE Convention. Philadelphia, 23 Nov. 1986.

GIROUX, HENRY A. Introduction. *The Politics of Education.* Freire xi–xxv.

———. *Theory and Resistance in Education: A Pedagogy for the Opposition.* Granby, MA: Bergin and Garvey Publishers, Inc., 1983.

GOELMAN, HILLEL, ANTOINETTE OBERG, and FRANK SMITH, eds. *Awakening to Literacy.* London: Heinemann, 1984.

GOODY, JACK, and IAN WATT. "The Consequences of Literacy." *Language and Social Context.* Ed. Pier Paolo Giglioli. New York: Penguin Books, 1972.

HABERMAS, JURGEN. *Theory and Practice.* Trans. John Viertel. Boston: Beacon Press, 1973.

HACKER, ANDREW. "Getting Rough on the Poor." *The New York Review of Books.* 13 October 1988: 12–17

Halfway Home and a Long Way to Go: Report of the 1986 Commission on the Future of the South. Southern Growth Policies Board. Durham, NC: Research Triangle Park, 1986.

HALLIDAY, M. A. K. *Learning How to Mean: Explorations in the Development of Language.* New York: Elsevier North Holland, 1975.

HAMRIN, ROBERT D. "Sorry Americans—You're Still Not 'Better Off'." *Challenge: Magazine of Economic Affairs.* 31 (Sept/Oct 1988): 50-51.

HARPER, ROB. "S. C. Breaks Through SAT Ranking." *South Carolina Schools.* 40 (September 1989): 1–3.

HARRINGTON, MICHAEL. *The New American Poverty.* New York: Holt, Rinehart & Winston, 1984.

——. *The Other America: Poverty in the United States.* New York: Penguin Books, 1983; Macmillan, 1962.

HAVELOCK, ERIC A. "The Alphabetization of Homer." *Communications Arts in the Ancient World.* Eds. Eric A. Havelock and Jackson P. Hershbell. New York: Hasting House Publishers, 1978. 3–21.

——. *Preface to Plato.* New York: Grossett and Dunlap, 1967.

HEATH, SHIRLEY BRICE. "The Achievement of Preschool Literacy for Mother and Child." Goelman, Oberg, and Smith 51–72.

——. "Toward an Ethnohistory of Writing in American Education." Whiteman 25–45.

——. *Ways with Words: Language, Life and Work in Communities and Classrooms.* New York: Cambridge UP, 1983.

——. "Will the Schools Survive?" Address to the closing General Session. NCTE. St. Louis, Missouri. November 1988.

HECHINGER, FRED. "Minority Teacher Plan Aims for Excellence." *New York Times.* 6 November 1984, Y20.

HEILBRONER, ROBERT L. *The Nature and Logic of Capitalism.* New York: W. W. Norton and Company, 1985.

HIGGINS, PEGGY. "Family, Job Hopes Spur Efforts to Learn to Read." *The Evening Herald.* Rock Hill, SC. 24 July 1985: A1+.

HIRSCH, E. D., JR. *The Philosophy of Composition.* Chicago: The University of Chicago Press, 1977.

——. *Cultural Literacy: What Every American Needs to Know.* Boston: Houghton Mifflin Company, 1987.

HOGGART, RICHARD. *The Uses of Literacy.* London: Pelican Books, 1948.

HOLT, JOHN. *How Children Fail.* New York: A Delta Book, Dell Publishing, 1964.

HOLZMAN, MICHAEL. "The Social Context of Literacy Education." *College English* 48 (1986): 27–33 and Cooper and Holzman 133.

HOLZMAN, MICHAEL, and OLGA CONNELLY. *Workplace Literacy: The Model Literacy Project, A Report to the California Conservation Corps.* Los Angeles: University of Southern California, 1984.

HOSKIN, KEITH. "Cobwebs to Catch Flies: Writing (and) the Child." Unpublished essay, Department of Education, University of Warwick, January 1984.

————. "The Examination, Disciplinary Power and Rational Schooling." *History of Education* 8.2 (1979): 135–146.

————. "The History of Education and the History of Writing." Unpublished Essay, Department of Education, University of Warwick, 1981.

HUNTER, CARMAN ST. JOHN, and DAVID HARMAN. *Adult Illiteracy in the United States: A Report to the Ford Foundation.* New York: McGraw-Hill, 1979.

IRMSCHER, WILLIAM. "Meditations on a Professional Organization." Inaugural Address to NCTE Convention. 21 Nov. 1983. Excerpted in *College English* 45 (1983): 53–57.

JENCKS, CHRISTOPHER. *Inequality, A Reassessment of the Effect of Family and Schooling in America.* New York: Basic Books, Inc., Publishers, 1972.

JOHNSON, DALE L., ed. *Class and Social Development: A New Theory of the Middle Class.* Beverly Hills: Sage Publications, 1982.

JOHNSON, DALE, and CHRISTIN O'DONNELL. "The Dequalification of Technical, Administrative, and Professional Labor." Johnson 225–244.

JORDAN, JUNE. "Problems of Language in a Democratic State." Keynote Address. NCTE Convention. Washington, D. C., 21 Nov. 1983.

————. "Nothing Mean More to Me Than You and the Future Life of Willie Jordan." *Harvard Education Review* 58 (August 1988): 363–374.

KAHL, JOSEPH A. *The American Class Structure.* New York: Holt, Rinehart and Winston, 1964.

KANTOR, KENNETH J., DAN R. KIRBY, and JUDITH P. GOETZ. "Research in Context: Ethnographic Studies in English Education." *Research in the Teaching of English* 15 (1982): 293–309.

KEATING, PAMELA, and JEANNIE OAKES. "Access to Knowledge: Breaking Down Barriers to Learning." *Access to Knowledge: Removing School Barriers to Learning. Youth At Risk.* Denver: The Education Commission of the States, 1988.

KINTSCH, WALTER, and TEUN A. VAN DIJK. "Toward a Model of Text Comprehension and Production." *Psychological Review* 85 (1978): 363–393.

"Kitchen Spanish." Published by Leslie Hayden. Insert. *Harper's Magazine.* March 1988: 24.

KOPKIND, ANDREW. "The Age of Reaganism, A Man and a Movement." *The Nation.* 239.14 (1984): 448+.

KOZOL, JONATHAN. *Illiterate America*. New York: Anchor/Doubleday Press, 1985.

KRAUS, KARL. *In These Great Times: A Karl Kraus Reader*. Trans. Joseph Fabry et al. Ed. Harry Zohn. Manchester: Carcanet, 1985.

LABOV, WILLIAM. *Language in the Inner City: Studies in the Black English Vernacular*. Philadelphia: University of Pennsylvania Press, 1972.

LANHAM, RICHARD. *Literacy and the Survival of Humanism*. New Haven: Yale UP, 1983.

―――. "Composition, Literature, and the Lower Division Gyroscope." *Profession* 84. New York: MLA of America, 1984. 10–15.

LEESON, LEE. California Conservation Corps Staff Development Literacy Workshops: Project Analysis. University of Southern California, Los Angeles, November 1985.

LENSKI, GERARD. *Power and Privilege: A Theory of Social Stratification*. McGraw-Hill, 1966.

LEVITAS, MAURICE. *Marxist Perspectives in the Sociology of Education*. London: Routledge and Kegan Paul, 1974.

LEWIS, MICHAEL. "Program sends mixed signals." *The State* (Columbia, SC). 30 October 1988. 1D.

LEWONTIN, R. C., STEVEN ROSE, and LEON J. KAMIN. *Not in Our Genes: Biology, Ideology and Human Nature*. New York: Pantheon Books, 1984.

Literacy Volunteers of America. National newspaper ad campaign. 1988.

"Low exit test scores." Editorial. *The State*. 12 October 1986, B2.

LUNSFORD, ANDREA. "Cognitive Development and the Basic Writer." *College English* 41 (1979): 38–46.

―――. "The Content of Basic Writer's Essays." *College Composition and Communication* 31 (1980): 278–290.

LURIA, A. R. *Cognitive Development: Its Cultural and Social Foundations*. ed. Michael Cole. Cambridge: Harvard UP, 1976.

LYND, ROBERT S., and HELEN MERRELL LYND. *Middletown: A Study in American Culture*. New York: Harcourt, Brace and World, Inc., 1929.

―――. *Middletown in Transition: A Study in Cultural Conflicts*. New York: Harcourt, Brace and Company, 1937.

MACKILLOP, JANE. *Ethnic Minorities in Sheffield*. City of Sheffield Adult Education Department, n.d.

MARCUS, RUTH. "Virginia's Innovative 'No Read, No Release' Parole Plan Is Not Without Critics." *The Washington Post* 23 February 1986: B1+.

MARCUSE, HERBERT. *One Dimensional Man*. Boston: Beacon Press, 1964.

MARTIN, NANCY. *Mostly About Writing.* Selected Essays. Portsmouth, NH: Boynton/Cook, 1983.

MARX, KARL, and FREDERIC ENGELS. *Selected Works in One Volume.* London: Lawrence and Wishart, 1968.

MCLUHAN, HERBERT MARSHALL. *The Gutenberg Galaxy: The Making of Typographic Man.* Toronto: University of Toronto Press, 1962.

MEDWAY, PETER. *Finding a Language: Autonomy and Learning in School.* London: Chameleon Educational Press, 1981.

MEEK, MARGARET, et al. *Achieving Literacy: Longitudinal Studies of Adolescents Learning to Read.* London: Routledge and Kegan Paul, 1983.

MOFFETT, JAMES. *Coming on Center: English Education in Evolution.* Portsmouth, NH: Boynton/Cook, 1981.

MORLAND, JOHN KENNETH. *Millways of Kent.* New Haven: College and University Press 1964; University of North Carolina Press, 1958.

MYRDAL, GUNNAR. *An American Dilemma: The Negro Problem and Modern Democracy.* Vol. 1. New York: Pantheon Books, A Division of Random House, 1962.

A Nation at Risk: The Imperative for Education and Reform. U. S. National Commission on Excellence in Education. GPO: 1983.

National Institute of Education. *Involvement in Learning: Realizing the Potential of American Higher Education.* Final Report of the Study Group on the Conditions of Excellence in American Higher Education. U. S. Department of Education, Washington, DC, 1984.

NORTON, JOHN, and JIM REX. Education Ground Paper. South Carolina Assembly on the Future. No date. [1988]

"Number of Blacks Taking SAT Drops 5 Pct. in 5 Years." *The Chronicle of Higher Education.* 3 September 1986: 108.

ONG, WALTER, J., S. J. "Reading, Technology, and Human Consciousness." Raymond 170–201.

OPPENHEIMER, MARTIN, CHRISTIN O'DONNELL, and DALE JOHNSON. "Professionalization/Deprofessionalization." Johnson 245–257.

PARKIN, FRANK. *Class Inequality and Political Order: Social Stratification in Capitalist and Communist Societies.* New York: Holt, Rinehart & Winston, 1971.

PERELMAN, CHAIM, and L. OLBRECHTS-TYTECA. *The New Rhetoric: A Treatise on Argumentation.* Trans. John Wilkinson and Purcell Weaver. Notre Dame: University of Notre Dame Press, 1966.

PERRY, THELMA. *History of the American Teachers Association.* Washington, DC: National Education Association, 1975.

PINES, BURTON YALE. *Back to Basics: The Traditionalist Movement That Is Sweeping Grassroots America.* New York: Morrow, 1982.

POSTER, MARK. *Existential Marxism in Postwar France, From Sartre to Althusser.* Princeton: Princeton UP, 1975.

———. *Foucault, Marxism and History. Mode of Production versus Mode of Information.* Cambridge: Polity Press, 1984.

POSTMAN, NEIL. "The Information Environment." *A Review of General Semantics* 36 (1979): 234–245.

———. "The New Literacy." *Grade Teacher* 88 (1971): 26–52.

POULANTZAS, NICOS. *Classes in Contemporary Capitalism.* Trans. David Fernbach. London: Verso, 1978.

POWER, SARAH GODDARD. "The Politics of Literacy." Bailey and Fosheim 21–29.

The Program in Writing at the Bread Loaf School of English. Middlebury, VT: Middlebury College, 1986.

Public Agenda Foundation. *Priorities for the Nation's Schools.* National Issues Forum. Dayton, OH: 1983.

Rankings of the Counties and School Districts of South Carolina 1986–87. SC: South Carolina Department of Education, 1988.

RASPBERRY, WILLIAM. "Standard English Should Be Required." *The State* (Columbia, SC). 7 October 1986: 12A.

RAYMOND, JAMES, ed. *Literacy as a Human Problem.* Tuscaloosa, AL: The University of Alabama Press, 1982.

RICHARDSON, EVE. "Dixie Goswami: A Teacher's Teacher; Dixie and the Bread Loaf." *The State Magazine,* supplement to *The State* (Columbia, SC). 2 March 1986: 8–10.

RIST, RAY C. "Blietzkrieg Ethnography: On the Transformation of a Method into a Movement." *Educational Researcher* 9.2 (1980): 8–10.

ROBINSON, JAY L. "Literacy in the Department of English." *College English.* 47 (1985): 482–498.

———. "What Is Literacy?" *Federation Review: The Journal of the State Humanities Councils* 8.4 (1985): 1–5.

RODBY, JUDITH. Literacy "Spikes": A Report Documenting and Evaluating the 1985 California Conservation Corps Corpsmember Literacy Workshops. University of California, Santa Barbara, 1985.

———. Literacy-Work Exchange Program: A Report Documenting and Evaluating the California Conservation Corps Literacy Workshops in Coordination with The California State University at San Diego, 1986.

ROSE, MIKE. *Writer's Block: The Cognitive Dimension.* Carbondale: Southern Illinois UP, 1984.

ROSEN, HAROLD. *The Language Monitors.* Bedford Way Papers 11. London: Institute of Education, University of London, 1982.

———. "Language and Social Class, A Critical Look at the Theories of Bernstein." London: Falling Wall Press, 1974.

ROSEN, HAROLD, and CONNIE ROSEN. *The Language of Primary School Children.* London: Penguin Books for the Schools Council, 1973.

ROTHMAN, ROBERT. "In 25 Years, Little Has Changed on Schools' Reading Lists." *Education Week.* 8 (7 June 1989): 6.

SADLER, TONI. "Group Closer to Fighting Illiteracy." *The Herald.* 21 July 1987, A3.

SARTRE, JEAN-PAUL. *Existentialism and Human Emotions.* New York: The Wisdom Library, 1957.

SCHIEFFELIN, BAMBI B., and MARILYN COCHRAN-SMITH. "Learning to Read Culturally: Literacy Before Schooling." Goelman, Oberg and Smith 3–23.

SCRIBNER, SYLVIA, and MICHAEL COLE. *The Psychology of Literacy.* Cambridge: Harvard UP, 1981.

SENNETT, RICHARD, and JONATHAN COBB. *The Hidden Injuries of Class.* New York: Vintage Books, Random House, 1973.

SERRIN, WILLIAM. "A Great American Job Machine?" *The Nation.* 18 September 1989: 269–272.

SEXTON, PORTER. "Catching the Right Bus for Educational Reform." *The College Board Review.* No. 148 (Summer 1988): 2–5, 36.

SHAUGHNESSY, MINA. *Errors and Expectations.* New York: Oxford UP, 1977.

SHAULL, RICHARD. Foreword. *Pedagogy of the Oppressed.* By Paulo Freire. 9–15.

SILBERMAN, CHARLES E. *Crisis in the Classroom: The Remaking of American Education.* New York: Random House, 1970.

SIMON, JOHN. *Paradigms Lost, Reflections on Literacy and Its Decline.* New York: Penguin Books, 1984.

SIZER, THEODORE R. *The Dilemma of The American High School.* The First Report from a Study of High Schools. Boston: Houghton Mifflin, 1984.

———. *Horace's Compromise: The Dilemma of the American High School.* Boston: Houghton Mifflin, 1984.

SKUBE, MICHAEL. "Black English Imprisons Blacks." *The Herald.* Rock Hill, SC. 27 August 1989: 3D

SLEDD, ANDREW. "Readin' not Riotin': The Politics of Literacy." *College English.* 50 (Sept. 1988), 495–508.

SLEDD, JAMES. "In Defense of the Students' Right." *College English* 45 (1983): 667–675.

———. "Doublespeak: Dialectology in the Service of Big Brother." *College English* 33 (1972): 439–456.

———. "On Not Teaching English Usage. *English Journal* 54 (1965): 698–703.

SMITH, FRANK. *Essays into Literacy.* Portsmouth, NH: Heinemann, 1984.

———. Introduction. Goelman, Oberg, and Smith v–xv.

SMITH, STEVE. "At risk students need attention." *The State*. 6 September 1987, B4.

———. "State board declares war on dropout rate." *The State*. 10 February 1989, B1.

SPONHOUR, MICHAEL. "Exit exam taking toll on 4,042 seniors." *The State*. 17 February 1990, A1.

"Statistics in Public Elementary and Secondary Education: From the 1987 Common Core Data." *ERS Spectrum: Journal of School Research and Information*. 7:2 (1989): 41–46.

STEINER, GEORGE. *After Babel: Aspects of Language and Translation*. London: Oxford UP, 1975.

———. "Books in an Age of Post Literacy." R. R. Bowker Memorial Lecture, New York City, 1984. (Reprinted in *Harper's*, "The Future of Reading," August 1985: 21–24).

STREET, BRIAN V. *Literacy in Theory and Practice*. Cambridge: Cambridge UP, 1984.

STRACENER, WILLIAM. "Election Official Envisions SC Voting by Computer." *The Charlotte Observer* 8 September 1985, South Carolina edition: C1.

STUCKEY, J. ELSPETH. "The Del Norte Model Literacy Program." Holzman and Connelly, N. pag.

———. "The USC Literacy Spike, May 1984." Holzman and Connelly, N. pag.

SUCHETKA, DIANE. "Older Students Help Younger Ones in Class." *York Observer*. Supplement to *The Charlotte Observer*. 20 October 1985, South Carolina edition: 5–6.

SZWED, JOHN F. "The Ethnography of Literacy." Whiteman 14–24.

TANNEN, DEBORAH. "Oral and Literate Strategies in Spoken and Written Discourse." Bailey and Fosheim 79–96.

———. "Oral and Literate Strategies in Spoken and Written Narratives." *Language* 58 (1982): 1–21.

THOMAS, LEWIS. *The Lives of a Cell: Notes of a Biology Watcher*. New York: Viking Press, 1974.

TISDALL, SIMON. "Poverty Timebomb Ticks on in US Cities." *The Guardian*. 6 February 1990: 4.

TORBE, MIKE and PETER MEDWAY. *The Climate for Learning*. Portsmouth, NH: Boynton/Cook, 1981.

To Secure the Blessings of Liberty. Report of the National Commission on the Role and Future of State Colleges and Universities. Washington, DC: American Association of State Colleges and Universities, 1986.

"Twenty Percent of Adults Can't Read." *The State* (Columbia, SC) 20 March 1986, C2.

United States Department of Education. *A Nation at Risk: The Imperative for Educational Reform.* By The National Commission on Excellence in Education. Washington, DC: GPO, 1983.

VOLOSINOV, V. N. *Marxism and the Philosophy of Language.* Trans. Ladislav Matejka and I. R. Titunik. New York: Seminar Press, 1973.

VYGOTSKY, LEV. *Thought and Language.* Cambridge: MIT Press, 1962.

WATT, IAN. *The Rise of the Novel: Studies in Defoe, Richardson and Fielding.* Berkeley: University of California Press, 1971.

WEBER, MAX. *The Methodology of the Social Sciences.* Trans. and Ed. Edward A. Shils and Henry A. Fitch. New York: The Free Press, 1968.

WELLS, SUSAN. "Vygotsky Reads Capital." *Correspondence Two.* Portsmouth, NH: Boynton/Cook, April 1985, N. Pag.

WHITEMAN, MARCIA FARR, ed. *Writing: The Nature, Development, and Teaching of Written Communication.* Vol. 1 of Variation in Writing: Functional and Linguistic-Cultural Differences. Hillsdale, NJ: Lawrence Erlbaum Associates, Publishers, 1981.

WICHE Projections Methodology. WICHE (Western Interstate Commission for Higher Education). Boulder, Colorado. 1985.

WILDEN, ANTHONY. *System and Structure: Essays in Communication and Exchange.* 2nd ed. London: Tavistock Publications, 1980.

"Will Books Survive?" *Harper's.* Forum. August 1985: 35–44.

WILLIAMS, CAROL. "Changing American Families: Challenges and Opportunities." Testimony before Human Resources Comittee. Commission on the Future of the South. 30 May 1986: 1–19.

WILLIAMS, JOSEPH M. *Style, Ten Lessons in Clarity and Grace.* Glenview, IL: Scott, Foresman, 1981.

WILLIS, PAUL E. *Learning to Labour: How Working Class Kids Get Working Class Jobs.* Great Britain: Gower, 1977.

WILKINS, ROGER. "Smiling Racism." *The Nation* 239 (1984): 455.